Endorsements

THE missing element in our exposition of holy Scripture is our failure to interpret the Bible in light of its Jewish origins. This is especially true of the New Testament. Now, Sean Emslie has expertly bridged that gap with his commentary on the lovely little book on Philippians.
—Dr. Dewey Bertolini, Teaching Shepherd, Safe Haven

Emslie writes in plain easy to understand prose as he depicts Paul as squarely within a Jewish mindset and yet a bridge to the uncircumcised at Phillipi.
—Rabbi Elliot Klayman, COO, Messianic Jewish Theological Institute

An essential resource for reading, discussing, teaching, and preaching Philippians within the Messianic Jewish community and beyond.
—Rabbi Russ Resnik, Rabbinic Counsel, Union of Messianic Jewish Congregations

Written in clear prose that renders accessible a new Messianic Jewish understanding of Paul that converges in fascinating ways with the "Paul within Judaism Perspective."
—Isaac W. Oliver, Associate Professor in Religious Studies, Bradley University

An important contribution to the emerging field of Messianic Jewish commentaries on the Bible.
—Anne K. Knafl, Ph.D., The University of Chicago Library

Represents a significant resource for those who recognize the importance and relevance of Paul's Jewish upbringing, training and perspective.
—Daniel Nessim, Chosen People Ministries

This commentary will be a welcome addition to the libraries of both scholar and lay person alike.
—Dr. Eli Lizorkin-Eyzenberg, President, Israel Bible Center

R. Sean Emslie has provided us a special gift in his commentary on Philippians.
—Daniel C. Juster, Th. D., Restoration from Zion of Tikkun Global

Having known Sean for decades, I can attest that Philippians is the perfect book upon which he should comment because like Sean, the book is richly relational.
—Rabbi Stuart Dauermann, PhD; Director, Interfaithfulness

For anyone who is interested in engaging Philippians through a Jewish lens, Emslie's commentary is an exceptional resource.
—Dr. Jennifer M. Rosner, Affiliate Assistant Professor of Systematic Theology at Fuller Theological Seminary

It is a good commentary on Philippians which is not an easy letter to comment upon. The commentary was presented in a nice readable form.

I particularly liked the references to Mark Nanos' works and thoughts on the given matters, including on the identity of "the dogs" in Philippians 3.

Emslie did a nice job of dealing with relevant Greek words & phrases. I enjoyed the commentary and wish Sean all the best with its future.
—Rabbi Dr. D. Friedman; Director, Bet Midrash Lev Zion Jerusalem, Israel

A MESSIANIC COMMENTARY

PAUL PRESENTS TO THE

PHILIPPIANS

UNITY IN THE MESSIANIC COMMUNITY

A MESSIANIC COMMENTARY

PAUL PRESENTS TO THE

PHILIPPIANS

UNITY IN THE MESSIANIC COMMUNITY

R. SEAN EMSLIE

Lederer Books
An imprint of
Messianic Jewish Publishers
Clarksville, MD 21029

1   2019

ISBN 978-1733935432

Library of Congress Control Number:2019943842

Published by
Lederer Books
An imprint of Messianic Jewish Publishers
6120 Day Long Lane
Clarksville, Maryland 21029

Distributed by
Messianic Jewish Resources Int'l.
www.messianicjewish.net
Individual and Trade Order line: 800-410-7647

Email: lederer@messianicjewish.net

Printed in the United States of America

For my beloved grandmother,
Vestel Gibson Manskar, of blessed memory.
She loved her Messiah, loved people, and loved to read the Bible.
I am honored to have been granted the first
18 years of my life with her.

"The world was not worthy of *her*!"
(Hebrews 11:38a)

Acknowledgments

Without Dr. David H. Stern's pioneering work in Messianic Jewish biblical interpretation through his *Jewish New Testament* and *Jewish New Testament Commentary*, my Philippians commentary would not have been written. It is an honor to know Dr. Stern and his wife, Martha, who have immeasurably inspired me in my Messianic life and work.

My deep thanks go to Rabbi Barry Rubin and Messianic Jewish Publishers for publishing this commentary and for developing a complete collection of Messianic commentaries on the *B'rit Hadashah* (New Testament).

This commentary grew out of my midweek Bible study at Ahavat Zion Messianic Jewish Synagogue. I am grateful to Rabbi Joshua Brumbach for encouraging me to teach the study and to subsequently write the commentary. I also appreciate my Bible-study students for their input, love, and support.

One of those students was award-winning writer and editor Susan Silver, who deserves much praise as she thoughtfully, diligently, and skillfully edited my manuscript, transforming it from a piece of coal into a diamond.

I am thankful for my dear friend and mentor Pastor Dewey Bertolini, who has been a great source of encouragement throughout this writing project and my ministry career.

Pastor Paul Brown graciously gave me his sermon notes from years of preaching on Philippians and also access to resource materials from the library of Bridge Bible Fellowship.

With Dr. Mark Nanos' monumental work *The Mystery of Romans,* I began my foray into "Paul within Judaism" studies years before the term was coined. I am honored to contribute to the genre of literature that Dr. Nanos created 22 years ago. He also played an important role in providing resources that were especially helpful in interpreting Philippians 3.

Of the Messianic Jewish thinkers of my lifetime, I am honored to have learned from and been mentored by Rabbi Dr. Stuart Dauermann, Rabbi Dr. Mark Kinzer, and Rabbi Dr. Carl Kinbar. I am thankful for their important role in molding my understanding of Messianic Jewish theology and biblical interpretation.

Finally, I want to express my deepest gratitude and love to my family for supporting me in this project.

CONTENTS

GENERAL EDITOR'S PREFACE xiii

FOREWORD xv

PREFACE 1

BACKGROUND TO THE LETTER TO THE PHILIPPIANS 3

The Letter 9

PHILIPPIANS 1 13

Chapter Introduction. 13

Commentary 14

Opening Greetings (1:1-2). 14

Thankfulness and Prayer for the Philippians (1:3-11). 23

Paul in Chains and the Spread of the Gospel (1:12–14) 29

Proclaiming the Messiah out of Jealousy (1:15–20) 31

To Live or Die? (1:21–26). 34

Walking Worthy Lives (1:27-30). 39

PHILIPPIANS 2 43

Chapter Introduction. 43

Commentary 44

To Model the Messiah (2:1–4). 44

The Messianic Hymn (2:5–11) 46

Paul's Call to Living the New Life in Messiah (2:12-18) 75

The Examples of Timothy and Epaphroditus (2:19-30) 81

The Example of Timothy (2:19–24) 81

The Example of Epaphroditus (2:25–30) 82

PHILIPPIANS 3 85

   Chapter Introduction. 85

   Commentary 86

      Conclusion? (3:1). 86

      Paul's Opponents (3:2–3) 87

      Paul's Response to the Opponents (3:4–11) 97

      The New Life in Messiah (3:12–17) 109

      The Way of Destruction (3:18–19) 111

      The Way of Life (3:20-21). 114

PHILIPPIANS 4 117

   Chapter Introduction. 117

   Commentary 118

      Closing Words (4:1). 118

      Disunity in the Community (4:2–3). 118

      Living in Union with Messiah (4:4–6) 122

      Call to Stand Firm in Their Faith (4:7-9). 123

      Love and Thankfulness for the Philippians (4:10–18). 125

      Words of Blessing and Encouragement (4:19–23) 129

GLOSSARY 131

BIBLIOGRAPHY 133

ABOUT THE AUTHOR 149

General Editor's Preface

Nearly all bible commentators emphasize the importance of understanding the historical, cultural and grammatical aspects of any text of scripture. As has been said, "A text without a context is a pretext." In other words, to assume one can understand what God has revealed through those who present his word— prophets, poets, visionaries, apostles— without knowing the context is presumption. To really understand God's word, it's essential to know something about who wrote it and to whom, what was actually said and what it originally meant, when, where, and why it was written.

By now, everyone knows that the New Testament is a thoroughly Jewish book, written nearly entirely by Jews, taking place in and around Israel. The people written about—Paul, Peter, James, John, etc.—were almost all Jews who never abandoned their identities or people. The topics covered—sin, salvation, resurrection, Torah, Sabbath, how to "walk with God," the Millennium, etc.—were all Jewish topics that came from the Hebrew scripture. The expressions used often were Jewish idioms of that day.

So, to fully understand the New Testament, it must be viewed through "Jewish eyes," meaning that the Jewish historical, cultural, grammatical must be examined.

There are commentaries for women, for men, for teens, even for children. There are commentaries that focus on financial issues in the bible. Others provide archaeological material. Some commentaries are topical. Others are the works of eminent men and women of

God. But, until now, no commentary series has closely looked at the Jewish context of the New Testament books.

In this series, we have invited some of the top Messianic Jewish theologians in the world to contribute their knowledge and understanding. Each has written on a book (or more) of the New Testament they've specialized in, making sure to present the Jewish aspects—the original context—of each book. These works are not meant to be a verse-by-verse exegetical commentary. There are already many excellent ones available. But, these commentaries supplement what others lack, by virtue of the fact they focus on the Jewish aspects.

A number of different authors wrote these commentaries, each in his own style. Just as the Gospels were written by four different men, each with his own perspective and style, these volumes, too, have variations. We didn't want the writers to have to conform too much to any particular style guide, other than our basic one.

You may see some Hebrew expressions or Hebrew transliterations of the names in the New Testament. Thus, one writer might refer to the Apostle to the Gentiles as Paul. Another might write, Shaul, Paul's Hebrew name. Still, another might write Saul, an Anglicized version of Shaul. And some might write Saul/Paul, to reflect, not reject the different ways this servant of Messiah was known.

Another variation is the amount of reference material. Some have ample footnotes or endnotes, while others incorporate references within the text. Some don't have an enormous amount of notes, based on the book for which they are writing commentary.

So, I invite you to put on your Jewish glasses (if you're not Jewish) and take a look at the New Testament in a way that will truly open up new understanding for you, as you get to know the God of Israel and his Messiah better.

Rabbi Barry Rubin
General Editor and Publisher

FOREWORD

Paul's letter to the Philippians, with its combination of warmth and intimacy, theological innovation and exploration, practical instruction and encouragement has often not received the attention it deserves. Yet its message of joyful testimony and its vision of Yeshua as humble servant and glorious king is particularly relevant to the modern movement of Jewish disciples of Yeshua known as Messianic Judaism. Its exposition of the suffering of the Messiah, the role Paul's own experience of prison and the nature of his *B'sorah* (Gospel) have much to teach Messianic Jews and Christians today. Just as the letter addressed the needs and problems in the 'ekklesia* (church) at Philippi then, so they speak powerfully and relevantly to us today.

Few have focused on its significant teaching on Torah in the light of Yeshua the Messiah and how this is to be lived out in the community of disciples. While the book has always been a favourite for personal devotion and spiritual growth, the modern Messianic movement has yet to embrace the book as a key example of what it means to know Yeshua and learn from Paul's discipleship teaching found in the letter to the Philippians. Sean Emslie's commentary redresses this lack of attention, and rightly gives the book the place it deserves. He offers to Messianic Jews and everyone else a compelling and new reading of the book which speaks powerfully to the needs of a new generation of readers.

Of the myriad available commentaries on Paul's Letter to the Philippians, less than a handful are authored by Jewish disciples of Yeshua (Edersheim, Sapphir, Stern). Sean Emslie breaks new ground in what is the first post-supersessionist contribution from within the Messianic Movement, and the reader will not be disappointed.

Emslie marshals the fruits of modern scholarship, providing a reading of Philippians that is not only accessible to the modern reader, but draws together the research in recent years on the context and background of the letter, a new approach to Paul's own account of his role within Judaism, and a love for the Messiah Yeshua in all his divine majesty and servant's humility.

The need for such a commentary has long been apparent, as previous commentators have regularly posed a dualism between Paul's Jewish-ness and his "Jesus-ness," where the old Law-keeping Saul has been mistakenly compared and found lacking with the new "saved by Grace" law-free Paul. Emslie successfully integrates the two, following the insights of Nanos, Kinzer and others, whilst providing a compelling reading of the text, and making it accessible to the general reader looking for encouragement and edification in addition to good exegesis and theological interpretation.

As a young Jewish disciple of Yeshua I studied Lightfoot's classic commentary on Philippians (1868). Whilst it helped me unpack the poetry and depth of the work, and challenged my understanding of the nature of Yeshua as fully human and fully divine, the wisdom and encouragement I received from the commentary was somewhat marred by the implicit supersessionism and anti-Judaism I detected in the language and thought of the author. Other commentaries also shared the same weakness, and I longed for a commentary that did not take an adversarial stance to Paul's Jewishness or set up an imagined "wall of partition" between a later Judaism and Christianity. Emslie's commentary is the first to hold these elements together successfully. His commentary is both helpful and encouraging, scholarly and well researched, and brings the reader, whether Jewish, Christian or otherwise, a feast of insights, explanation and application that achieves Paul's own aim, to point to a life lived with Yeshua at the centre, and gives guidance and a model for achieving this.

What does it mean to be Jewish disciples of Rabbi Yeshua today? Emslie's commentary on this important book, an intimate letter from a 1st century rabbi and disciple of Rabbi Yeshua, points the way, and will be enjoyed by all who are interested in putting Yeshua's teaching into practice, and becoming more like Him today.

I warmly commend this book and am grateful to Sean for all that he has contributed in his studies and teaching to make it available to a wider audience.

Richard Harvey

Associate Lecturer
All Nations College

Preface

The idea for this commentary grew out of a four-week series on Philippians that I developed and taught for the Ahavat Zion Messianic Jewish Synagogue midweek Bible study (initially when Rabbi Joshua Brumbach was going to be away at conferences). At the conclusion of the series, Rabbi Brumbach suggested that I expand my notes from the class into a Messianic Jewish commentary on the letter.

Such a commentary will play a role in the vital work establishing a Messianic Jewish commentary series on the New Testament that Messianic Jewish Publishers has been developing over the last few years. Up to this time the only complete modern Messianic Jewish commentary on the New Testament has been Dr. David H. Stern's *Jewish New Testament Commentary*. Dr. Stern's monumental work is the foundation on which future commentaries and books highlighting the Messianic Jewish background of the New Testament will be built. Dr. Stern produced a one-volume work; I, along with other scholars, are expanding his work into individual, standalone volumes on each of the New Testament books.

Unlike much teaching on Paul within the Church and some branches of the Messianic world, this Philippians commentary sees the author not as Sha'ul the Jew becoming Paul the Christian or Paul the *Torah*-free Jew, but rather as Paul the Jew whose whole life was bound up and enlivened by his knowledge of and relationship with Yeshua.

This relationship ironically led the Jewish Paul to devoting his life to bringing the message of Yeshua (Hebrew for Jesus) to the Gentile world. In doing so, he gained greatly but he also relinquished his role as a rising star within Judaism who, like his mentor Gamaliel, could have become a prominent sage within Rabbinic Judaism; instead, he chose a path similar to that of his new master, Yeshua, which included suffering and execution.

While focusing on the primacy of the biblical text itself, i.e., the holy words of the living God via Paul the Apostle, this commentary also examines the Jewish background and Messianic Jewish theology inherent in the text, bringing new understandings to this important letter from Paul to the people of Philippi. Moreover, this commentary contributes to the literature of Messianic Jewish theology and biblical interpretation by focusing on the "Paul-within-Judaism" literature as well as post-supersessionist theology.

BACKGROUND TO THE LETTER TO THE PHILIPPIANS

But you will receive power when the Ruach HaKodesh comes upon you; you will be my witnesses both in Yerushalayim and in all Y'hudah and Shomron, indeed to the ends of the earth!

(Acts 1:8)

With these words, the mission to reach the world with the message of Yeshua began. Starting with Jerusalem and Judea, the message of Yeshua spread among the Jews of the Land. The earliest Messianic Community was a movement of Jews. With the message of Yeshua moving to the ends of the earth, the doors were opened to the Gentile world.

The earliest followers of Messianic Jewish faith understood themselves as a form of Judaism. Jewish scholar Jacob Neusner (*Judaisms* 139) even described such faith as one of the "Judaisms" of the Second Temple era. Early on a debate arose over Gentiles coming to Yeshua faith and their relationship to the *Torah* and Jewish practices, especially circumcision for men. This issue of debate in the early Messianic community became crucial in Acts 15:1 when men from Judah went to Antioch to teach the Gentile believers, "You can't be saved unless you undergo *b'rit-milah* in the manner prescribed by Moshe."

This teaching conflicted with Paul and Bar-Nabba's (Barabas') teachings to the Gentiles and led to an important decision by the early Messianic Jewish leadership group, which later became known as the Jerusalem Council (Acts 15:6ff). After hearing debate from both sides, Ya'akov (James), the brother of Yeshua and the leader of the Messianic Community in Jerusalem, suggested the following:

> Therefore, my opinion is that we should not put obstacles in the way of the Gentiles who are turning to God. Instead, we should write them a letter telling them to abstain from things polluted by idols, from fornication, from what is strangled and from blood (Acts 15:19–20).

Ya'akov's opinion about eliminating the "obstacles" of circumcision as well as *Torah* observance and substituting less stringent practices resulted in the council's unanimous ruling (Acts 15:25). The council then sent a letter to be read to all the Gentile communities declaring that Gentiles did not need to convert to Judaism nor to undergo male circumcision before becoming full members of the Messianic Community and followers of Yeshua.

This ruling supported two important truths that can be missed by modern scholars—be they Christian or Jewish.

First, the fact that gentile *Torah* observance, including circumcision, was an issue to the Messianic Community demonstrated the importance of continued *Torah* observance and practice of Judaism for the Messianic Jews. If, as many commentators suggest, this ruling ended *Torah* observance for *all* followers of Yeshua, both Jews and Gentiles, bringing this issue to the Jerusalem Council would have been a non-issue. If the Messianic Jews themselves had already decided to abandon *Torah* as Yeshua followers, it seems pointless and even cruel to require the Gentiles to honor *Torah* if the Jews had already abandoned it. The Acts account documenting the Jerusalem Council debate confirms *Torah* observance as an important part of Messianic Jewish faith rather than demonstrating an early abandonment of Jewish life and *Torah* observance of the earliest Yeshua believers.

Second, the Jerusalem Council asserted that Gentiles coming to Yeshua faith could and *should* come to Yeshua as Gentiles. This is the mystery of the Gospel that through Yeshua the way was open for Gentiles to join with the People of God but remain Gentiles. No longer would Gentiles need to convert to Judaism and observe circumcision for males and *Torah* observance for all, but now, by trusting in Yeshua, Gentiles could become part of the People of God as *Gentiles*.

The Jerusalem Council defended not only the unity of the now multinational People of God but also the distinct responsibilities and relationship to the *Torah* for Jews and Gentiles. For Jews, coming to Yeshua faith was accepting the Messiah of Israel promised in the *Tanakh* and continuing to live as Jews ordering their life according to *Torah* commands. Messianic Jews weren't abandoning Judaism and *Torah* but were embracing Israel's Messiah, which would include empowerment from the Spirit of God to grow in *Torah* living as Yeshua promised:

> If you love me, you will keep my commands; and I will ask the Father, and he will give you another comforting Counselor like me, the Spirit of Truth, to be with you forever. (John 14:15–16)

For Gentiles, coming to Yeshua faith was accepting the Messiah of Israel promised in the *Tanakh* and continuing to live as redeemed Gentiles. Unlike the Jewish followers of Yeshua, these Gentile Yeshua followers were not required to observe *Torah*-faithful lives, yet the Jerusalem Council provided basic ethical and moral commands as a start, with Apostolic teaching to further lead them to live as redeemed Gentiles. Thus, Gentiles were included into the Body of Messiah *as Gentiles* and did not require conversion to Judaism to be accepted.

The Jerusalem Council set the basis for what Kinzer (151) has called the "bilateral ecclesia": one Body of Messiah with two distinct ways of living Yeshua faith: the Jewish way of *Torah* observance for Messianic Jews and the Gentile way of freedom from *Torah* based solely on Yeshua faith. Such a model should be the basis for the twenty-first-century Body of Messiah as well: a Jewish, *Torah*-faithful Messianic Judaism and a multinational Christianity consisting of the faithful from the nations who trust in Yeshua and live unbound to *Torah* observance.

Rather than the unilateral views of all believers in Yeshua being free from the *Torah* as seen in much of the Church's teaching and the unilateral view of all Yeshua believers being subjected to *Torah* observance as held by "Hebrew Roots" groups, the Jerusalem Council ratified faith in one Messiah, Yeshua, for all and two ways of living Yeshua faith, one for Jews and one for Gentiles—distinct paths grounded in a unified faith.

Understood this way, the Jerusalem Council decision shows God's hand in both Judaism and Christianity and the unity our Messiah called both Jewish and Gentile followers to model while living as distinct communities and two important witnesses to our world: a Jewish Messianic Community and a Gentile Messianic Community.

The leaders of the Messianic Community in Jerusalem stated clearly that Gentiles coming to Yeshua faith did not need to become Jews first before accepting Yeshua as Messiah, which would have required ritual circumcision for males and *Torah* observance for males and females; instead, faith alone in the crucified and risen Yeshua was the only necessary entry step for those from the nations to join with the People of God, the Jewish people. Together they followed the God of Israel and opened up the message to the whole world.

With the issue of Gentiles coming to Yeshua faith as Gentiles resolved, Paul is ready to bring this newly endorsed statement to the cities he visited in his previous mission to Asia Minor (modern-day Turkey). In Acts 16, Paul received a vision that opened up the spread of the good news of Yeshua to Macedonia (modern-day Greece):

> There a vision appeared to Sha'ul at night. A man from Macedonia was standing and begging him, "Come over to Macedonia and help us!" As soon as he had seen the vision, we lost no time getting ready to leave for Macedonia; for we concluded that God had called us to proclaim the Good News to them. (Acts 16:9–10)

After experiencing this vision, Paul set out immediately to share the message of Yeshua with the people of Macedonia. In Acts 16:12, Paul comes to Philippi, a Roman colony and major city in Macedonia that was named after Phillip II, the father of Alexander the Great. Emperor Augustus declared Philippi's status as a Roman colony after Philippi had been the site of his and Mark Antony's victory over Brutus and Cassius, the lead assassins of Julius Caesar in 42 B.C.E. Later, near Philippi, Augustus would defeat Mark Antony in 31 B.C.E., which guaranteed his place as successor to Julius Caesar. Augustus named the city in honor of the Julian family, calling it Colonia Iulia Augusta Philippensis (Bockmuehl 3). Although the majority of the populace of Philippi was Greek, the administration and political hierarchy were held by Romans (Keown 36–37). The religion of Philippi included elements of Greek, Roman, Thracian, Egyptian, and other religions including hero worship and syncretic mixing of various religions (Hartog "Macedonia").

Unlike most of the cities that Paul would visit on his missionary journeys, Philippi does not appear to have had a large enough Jewish community to support an actual synagogue, which would have required at least ten Jewish men. According to Acts 16:13, those who met for prayer on *Shabbat* met at the riverside and the only worshippers mentioned were women. Interesting enough, Lydia, the one woman mentioned by name, is a "God-fearer," which could mean that the Jewish worshippers of Philippi may have been made up of God-fearers, Gentile adherents of Judaism, without a local Jewish population. It is also possible that some of these women were converts to Judaism, given that conversion to Judaism by Gentile women was easier as no circumcision was required, which resulted in more female conversions (Lieu 84). The following comments on Philippians 1:1 support this possibility:

> Without concluding too much from silence, these observations do lend a heightened significance to the unusual presence of an exclusively or at any rate predominantly female Sabbath congregation. This phenomenon may well correspond to the common numerical predominance of women among proselytes and god-fearers, due partly to the absence of circumcision as a deterrent and partly to the relatively more respected status of women within Judaism. (Bockmuehl 10)

The Messianic Community in Philippi began with Lydia and her household coming to believe in Yeshua (Acts 16:14-15). By the conclusion of Paul's first visit to Philippi (Acts 16:40), a group of Yeshua followers appears to be meeting at Lydia's house, which would be the beginning of the Philippian Messianic Community to whom Paul will send his letter.

The Letter

Paul wrote the Philippians letter from Rome probably in 62 C.E., during his final imprisonment as recorded in Acts 28:14–31. Philippians is one of four books written by Paul which are known as the Prison Epistles or Prison Letters, which include Ephesians, Philippians, Colossians, and Philemon. All four letters were written from prison and based on the above, it is held that all four letters were written from Paul's imprisonment in Rome, which we read about in Acts 28:30–31:

> Sha'ul remained two whole years in a place he rented for himself; and he continued receiving all who came to see him, openly and without hindrance proclaiming the Kingdom of God and teaching about Lord Yeshua the Messiah.

This final imprisonment before his execution by Nero was under a form of house arrest where he was confined to a rented room for the last two years of his life (Dobson 1506).

That Rome was the place of writing is based on the historic understanding from Church history up until the end of the eighteenth century (MacArthur 5) and also internal references in Philippians to "the whole palace" (1:13) and "the Emperor's household" (4:22). Also noteworthy is the severe nature of Paul's impending judgment mentioned in 1:19–23, where execution was a possibility, meaning he would be facing the Emperor as judge, making Rome the only location for the writing of the letter (MacArthur 6).

Some modern scholars such as N.T. Wright (*Resurrection* 225) have proposed either Caesarea or Ephesus as the locale for this letter. There are other scholars that understand the late nature of the letter, which also points to Rome, based on evidence from the letter including the more advanced Christology, for example Chapter 2's Messianic hymn, and also Paul's reference to elders and deacons, which would indicate a formalized ecclesiastical structure in Philippi, considered to be a later development in the Messianic communities that Paul planted (Boring 219). This commentary considers Rome to be the place of writing.

Many scholars believe that this letter is a combination of two or even three letters Paul sent to Philippi that had been edited into one letter (Fredriksen *Pagans* 63). A possible breakdown of the letter into three letters is seen as follows: the first letter as 4:10–20, Paul's thanks for the Philippians' gifts; a second as 1:1–3:1 and 4:4–7; 21–23, warning against division; and a third as 3:2–4:3;8–9, an attack on false teachers

(Carson and Moo 509). Carson and Moo's proposed three letters that are combined into our current one letter may seem odd. It is not three letters combined into one but sections of three letters combined together, as we see from the portions being from separate chapters of the current book. This can be understood as modern scholars seeing the three letters being written on one theme (Letter 1 on the Philippians gift, Letter 2 on division in the community that is covered in all 4 chapters of our current letter, and Letter 3 on false teachers that is the focus of chapters 3 and 4 of the letter). The Greek word that Paul used for "letter" is plural—"letters"—which can bolster those scholars and biblical interpreters who see Paul's Letter to the Philippians as a combination of letters to the Philippians (Roberts, Donaldson and Coxe 33).

In his Letter to the Philippians Paul took the common Hellenistic letter format and used it as a source of instruction and teaching in the early Messianic Community (Boring 197). In so doing Paul transformed a mode primarily of personal, secular communication into a tool for expanding the work of the Gospel and transmission of Messianic theology and thought.

As one of the early Church leaders and writers, Polycarp (who was also a student of the Apostle John), admired how Paul taught in person and through writing, which he interestingly wrote about in his own Philippian letter known as *The Epistle of Polycarp to the Philippians*:

> For neither I, nor any other such one, can come up to the wisdom of the blessed and glorified Paul. He, when among you, accurately and steadfastly taught the word of truth in the presence of those who were then alive. And when absent from you, he wrote you a letter. (Polycarp 33)

While originally targeted to particular congregations, Paul's letters also served as teaching tools for other communities, as we see documented in Paul's Letter to the Colossians where he instructs them to share their letter with the Messianic Community in Laodicea:

> After this letter has been read to you, have it read also in the congregation of the Laodiceans; and you, in turn, are to read the letter that will come from Laodicea. (Col. 4:16)

Moreover, nearly 2,000 years later, Paul's Letters are studied today and continue to teach each new generation of Yeshua followers.

Paul's letter reveals several main purposes and themes. First, Paul was motivated to write the Philippians to thank them for the gifts they had sent him upon hearing he was now in Rome (Dobson 1506). Second, Paul expressed gratitude for his relationship with the Philippians. The shared love of Paul for the Philippians and theirs for Paul defined their relationship. This mutual love is reflected in Paul's personal letter focusing on his encouragement of and thankfulness for dear friends in his life and ministry (Phil. 1:3–8). Within this personal context Paul writes openly about his imprisonment and lauds the work of Timothy and Epaphroditus on behalf of him for the Philippian Community.

Finally, building on the Philippians' closeness and mutual affection for Paul, he speaks to them as their spiritual leader, calling them to unity grounded in humility—the kind of humility exemplified in the life and death of Yeshua described in Philippians 2. Paul urged humility by the Philippians, calling them to unite as an example for Yeshua, thereby continuing to spread the Good News (Schreiner *Interpreting* 4).

PHILIPPIANS 1

For to me, life is the Messiah, and death is gain.
—Philippians 1:21

Chapter Introduction

In Chapter 1, Paul begins his letter to the Philippians sharing his deep love for this Messianic community. The love he has for the Philippians is grounded in their love for him and participation in his work of ministry.

Philippi was the first city in Europe that Paul brought the message of Yeshua (see Acts 16). With this launch into the primarily Gentile world, Paul called coming to Philippi "the early days of my work spreading the Good News, when I left Macedonia" (Phil. 4:15).

One of the most familiar verses of the letter is in this chapter, Philippians 1:21, where Paul stresses the centrality of Yeshua in his life. Paul's whole life from his encounter with Yeshua on the road to Damascus to his execution under Nero was all about knowing Messiah more and becoming, as he frequently said, to be "in Messiah." Paul will further discuss the centrality of Yeshua throughout the letter with this being the first and most direct affirmation of Yeshua being his source of life now and into eternity.

Commentary

Opening Greetings (1:1-2)

---

1 From: Sha'ul and Timothy, slaves of the Messiah Yeshua

To: All God's people united with the Messiah Yeshua and living in Philippi, along with the congregation leaders and shammashim [deacons]:

From: Sha'ul

The writer of this letter is the Apostle Paul, also known as Sha'ul. The Complete Jewish Bible uses the name "Sha'ul" for all references to Paul in the *B'rit Hadashah* (New Testament). Sha'ul was his Hebrew or "synagogue" name (Reumann 53) and like other Jews of the time, he also adopted a Greco-Roman second name, "Paulus," or in English, "Paul" (Deissmann 315–317). This second gentile name was usually chosen based on a similar sound or other relationship to the Hebrew name (O'Brien 44). A similar naming practice occurs today by gentiles who convert to Judaism or Jews who were not raised religiously when they adopt a Jewish name related to their birth name, for example, Reuben for Robert or Shoshanna for Susan.

Starting in Acts 13:9 we encounter Paul's two names: "Then Sha'ul, also known as Paul, filled with the *Ruach HaKodesh*, stared straight at him…" From this point forward in Acts, Luke refers to Sha'ul by his Greco-Roman name, "Paul"; also of note is that Paul refers to himself by this name in all of his letters (Betz, vol. 5 187). Throughout this commentary we will use the name "Paul," reflecting his own use and that of other source research materials.

This name change from Sha'ul to Paul in Acts could be understood as marking a shift of focus and field of service, from Sha'ul the Jewish disciple to Paul the Apostle of Messiah to the whole world, his globally recognized name reflecting his new global mission (Deissmann 315–317). This understanding is in contrast to the teaching that he changed his name from Sha'ul to Paul to demonstrate his rejection of Judaism and his life as a Jew to become Paul the Christian. In fact, as an educated Jew from the Pharisees, Paul would take his knowledge of the *Tanakh* and Jewish tradition to communicate the message about Yeshua to the Philippians (Das 3).

And Timothy

Timothy was one of Paul's most loyal coworkers who joined Paul as he was beginning his second missionary journey to the Asia Minor Messianic communities. The purpose of this journey was to share the rulings of the Jerusalem Council announcing that Gentiles could become members of the Messianic Community without first converting to Judaism. Timothy is introduced in Acts 16:1-4:

> "Sha'ul came down to Derbe and went on to Lystra, where there lived a *talmid* named Timothy. He was the son of a Jewish woman who had come to trust and a Greek father. All the brothers in Lystra and Iconium spoke well of Timothy. Sha'ul wanted Timothy to accompany him; so he took him and did a *b'rit-milah*, because of the Jews living

> in those areas; for they all knew that his father had been a
> Greek. As they went on through the towns, they delivered
> to the people the decisions reached by the emissaries and
> the elders in Yerushalayim for them to observe."

In this introduction, we see that Timothy was the son of a Greek father and a Jewish mother who had become a follower of Yeshua (and we will also learn in 2 Timothy 1:5 that his grandmother, Eunice, was also a Messianic Jew), making him a third-generation Messianic Jew). Though we do not know why Timothy was not circumcised, it appears from the text that his Greek father may have objected to having his son circumcised, possibly because of the Greek aesthetic ideal of not desecrating the perfect human form by removing foreskin. Perhaps, too, his father rejected what circumcision could mean for his son's identity: separation from Gentile society (by being circumcised and having a mark on the flesh to denote inclusion in the People of Israel) and distinction from the "uncircumcised" world (Schäfer 98).

To prevent any confusion over Timothy's status as a Jew or any issues among the Jewish communities and synagogues on their journey that could disrupt their Gospel work, Paul circumcised Timothy (Acts 16:3). Paul did not want Timothy's possibly ambiguous Jewish identity to pose a roadblock in the work of sharing their message among the Jewish populations of Asia Minor; the fact that Timothy was Jewish and uncircumcised would have caused a stumbling block to the mission of sharing the Jewish Messiah with fellow Jews (Stern, *Commentary* 283) .

Paul demonstrated Timothy's importance to him as a

coworker and disciple by mentioning Timothy in eight of his letters, and Timothy himself also received two of Paul's letters (Stern *Commentary* 593). Paul may have included Timothy in the greeting portion of letters to indicate that Timothy functioned as his secretary who physically wrote the letter as Paul dictated it to him (Thielman 347). Paul also endorsed Timothy's authority as a leader by including him in the opening greeting (Thielman 358).

Slaves of the Messiah Yeshua

Paul refers to himself and Timothy as "slaves of the Messiah." This self-identification is an essential precursor to one of the essential themes of the book, namely, that followers of Yeshua were to model Yeshua's humility and willingness to be a slave, a humble servant willing to give their life for the Messianic Community. Paul will use the Greek word for slave, δοῦλος (*doulos*), to refer to Yeshua later in Philippians 2:7 (Bockmuehl 50).

Given the nature of life in the Roman Empire and a major city such as Philippi, the Philippians would be familiar with slavery and what it meant in their society to be a slave. In the use of δοῦλοι (*douloi*) for "slaves" to represent himself and Timothy and later to refer to Yeshua as a δοῦλος (*doulos*) or "slave" in the Messianic hymn of Chapter 2, Paul is making clear to the Philippians what following Yeshua means and what the model for their new life entails (Thielman 348) .

The Theological Dictionary of the New Testament says that the word *doulos* meant that the service offered by the slave is performed out of submission and dependence on the master (Rengstorf, vol. 2 273). This description certainly applies to

Paul and Timothy who were entirely devoted to their master and Lord, Yeshua.

For Paul being a "slave" of Messiah Yeshua was a wholehearted, joyful act of submission to Yeshua as his Lord. Being a slave of Messiah was to Paul the realization of true freedom (Loh 5), as we see in Romans 6:22:

> However, now, freed from sin and enslaved to God, you do get the benefit—it consists in being made holy, set apart for God, and its end result is eternal life.

Paul's enslavement was no longer to sin and death but to Yeshua and life, both now and eternally. In his slavery to Yeshua he was truly free from enslavement to sin.

Though it was detrimental to call oneself a slave in Greek and Roman cultures, Paul here is teaching a lesson to the Philippians on the critical role of being considered a slave to the Messiah, echoing the use of "servant" as title of honor for someone chosen for service to the Lord in the *Tanakh* (Josh. 24:29; Ps. 89:20, Neh. 10:29) (Hansen 39). (In Greek, *doulos* is used for both "slave" and "servant.") The LXX (Septuagint), the Greek translation of the *Tanakh*, uses *doulos* in referring to Moses, Joshua, and David in the above verses. עֶבֶד (*eved*) is the Hebrew word that was translated as *doulos* in the above passages, making for a connection between the "slaves" of the *Tanakh* (Moses, Joshua, David, and others) with the "slaves" of the *B'rit Hadashah*—Paul, Timothy, and by their example, the believers in Philippi (Cousar 24).

Paul also makes clear that he is a slave of Yeshua the Jewish Messiah. His devotion to Yeshua is central to his self-identification. It is in finding and submitting himself to the Jewish Messiah that Paul sees meaning in his life, and he stated clearly here that his only proper response to his encounter with the Messiah is his subjection to him as a slave. His identification as a slave of Yeshua motivated him to model Yeshua and commend the same way of life to the Philippians (Hansen 3).

To: All God's people united with the Messiah Yeshua and living in Philippi

Paul wrote the letter to people in Philippi, a city in what is now the modern country of Greece. It was also the first city in Europe where Paul visited and established a Messianic Community (Stern, *Commentary* 593). As seen earlier, Philippi had a minimal Jewish population, so Paul was writing to a mostly Gentile Messianic Community, though there would have been some Jews and God-fearers who were members of the community.

The phrase "All God's people" is rendered "all God's holy people" in some other translations. The Greek word ἅγιος (*hagiois*), sometimes translated as "holy ones" or "saints," is used in the Septuagint to translate the Hebrew word קדוש (*kadosh*). Scholar Mark Nanos sees in the phrase "all God's holy people" Paul's continuing connection to Pharisaic Jewish life, holiness within that life, and his desire for the Philippians to be holy (*View* 177). He also understands that Paul is bringing these Gentiles in Philippi into a life of holiness, walking in a new way of life for them within the context of a Jewish understanding and framework for their Yeshua faith, even as they remain Gentiles.

Along with the congregation leaders and shammashim:

Paul makes a point to include in his opening words a greeting to both the congregational leaders and *shammashim* (deacons). In doing so, Paul is showing that there was an established leadership over the community in Philippi. Paul wanted to alert these leaders on their roles and responsibilities to learn from Paul as the overseer for all the Messianic communities and also teach the people under their spiritual care in Philippi to walk in God's ways.

The role of elders over a synagogue was familiar from Jewish practice. The original twelve *talmidim* (students, disciples) of Yeshua, who would have led in the early Messianic Community in Jerusalem, served a continuation of this established practice (Lightfoot 111). They were joined by Ya'akov (James), the brother of Yeshua, who became the leader of the Jerusalem Messianic Community. These elders were to be devoted to the spiritual needs of the Messianic Community (Acts 6:2) and to continue this focus, they chose *shammashim* dedicated to the physical demands of the Messianic Community (Acts 6:3-7). Paul in 1 Timothy 3:1–13 and Titus 1:6 gave a listing of requirements for those to be elders and *shammashim*.

We can see in Acts 14:23, from Paul's first missionary journey, that he established elders in the communities that he founded:

> After appointing elders for them in every congregation, Sha'ul and Bar-Nabba [Barnabas], with prayer and fasting, committed them to the Lord in whom they had put their trust.

From this example, we can understand that Paul and Timothy in Philippi, as recorded in Acts 16, would have chosen elders over the Messianic Community, which they began on their first trip to Philippi on Paul's Second Missionary Journey (Carson and Moo 28).

In referring to the congregational leaders in the greeting, Paul could be making them aware of his message to the community (especially in Paul's reference to false teachers and false teachings as described in Chapter 3:1–11). As spiritual leaders in the community, they were to stand for the truth of the Gospel and against false teaching like shepherds over a flock (Thielman 348). The leaders would also be called upon by Paul later in the book to deal with disunity among leaders (Phil. 4:2–3) which could fracture the whole community (Merida 16).

Also given that one of Paul's motivations for writing the letter was to thank the Philippians for their gifts to him (see Chapter 4), Paul here could be greeting the leaders of the community who were responsible for collecting and distributing the contributions of the Philippians to Paul (Loh 7).

Though a fully formed congregational leadership structure in the early Messianic communities is understood to be a later development (Carson and Moo 56), it appears from this greeting that, at least in Philippi, a congregational structure included congregational leaders and *shammashim*. Although this structure in Philippi was not a common organizational structure until the second century C.E. (Sanders *Paul* 594–595), some commentators have suggested this structure could have developed earlier in Philippi, based on their cultural desire for official leadership structure, from possibly a strong Roman influence (Bockmuehl 53). From Acts 16 and the Letter to the Philippians we learn of several leaders by name in the Philippian Messianic Community including Lydia, Euodia, Syntyche, Syzygus, Clement, and the other "fellow workers" of Paul (Boring 218).

---

2 Grace to you and shalom from God our Father and the Lord Yeshua the Messiah.

Grace to you and shalom

The standard greeting for Greek letters would have used the word χαίρειν (*chairein*), which means "greetings." In his letters Paul changes the word to χάρις (*charis*), which means "grace" (O'Brien 50). When Paul opens with grace over mere greetings, he immediately presents a core teaching of the Messianic faith. Paul also adds εἰρήνη (*eirene*), the Greek word used for the Hebrew word שלום (*shalom*), meaning "peace" in the LXX (Septuagint). Paul draws on the deep meaning of *shalom* in the *Tanakh* (the Old Testament), pointing to spiritual completeness or wholeness (Silva 38). By using these two greetings together, grace and peace, Paul could be sending the Philippians both a common Greek and a common Jewish greeting to begin his letter to this community of Gentile and Jewish Yeshua followers (Bockmuehl 56).

From God our Father and the Lord Yeshua the Messiah.

Paul completes the greeting, making clear to the Philippians that grace and *shalom* come from God the Father and the Lord Yeshua. I-Jin Loh and Eugene Nida (8) put it this way:

The ultimate source of grace and peace is obviously God, whom Jesus revealed as Abba Father, but to the extent that such blessing is made possible only through Jesus, who is confessed as Messiah (Christ the anointed King) and exalted as Lord by his resurrection (2:9), he too is to be acclaimed as the giver of grace and peace.

Some commentators have cautioned about making too much of the possible Christological implications of this phrase in the opening of the letter. In light of other Pauline writings, including the early Messianic hymn in Philippians 2:6–11, Paul acknowledges the divine nature of Yeshua and his eternal unity with God the Father and elsewhere with the Spirit of God to form the triune God (Fee *Letter* 71). Paul saw no problem in greeting the Philippians with a word that united Yeshua with the One God of Israel, here designated as the Father. It is the divine Son working in the world with the Father to fulfill the divine plan and bring grace and peace that Paul has in mind here, commending this knowledge to the Philippians (Fee *Letter* 71).

Beyond making an important theological point about the lordship and divine nature of Yeshua, Paul begins his letter with a significant and dangerous political declaration— that Yeshua is Lord, which was in contrast to the expected acknowledgment of Caesar as Lord (Merida 17).

Thankfulness and Prayer for the Philippians (1:3-11)

3 I thank my God every time I think of you.

In his letters to the Galatians and Corinthians Paul wrote using harsh terms to correct false teachings and sinful activities that plagued these Messianic communities; here in Philippians, however, Paul can warmly share his love and concern for the Philippians and make them aware of how thankful he is to God for them and their love for him and their work for the Messiah. As will be seen later in the letter, Paul has derived much joy from the Philippians and is thankful to God for their work for him in spreading the Good News. Paul also has good memories of how the Messianic Community in Philippi showed him love and care, and he focuses on these memories whenever he thinks of them (Merida 21).

---

4 Whenever I pray for all of you I always pray with joy,

Paul here uses the Greek word δεήσει (*deēsis*), usually translated as "supplication," to demonstrate his serious prayer for them (Loh 11). As apostle to the Gentiles, Paul is sharing how deeply he loves and seeks the best from God for them. Paul used the same Greek word *deēsis* in Romans 10:1, speaking about his heart for the Jewish People:

> Brothers, my heart's deepest desire and my prayer to God
> for Isra'el is for their salvation;

In using "all of you" in his prayers for the Philippians, Paul shows the importance of all the Philippian believers understanding their unity in Messiah and how vital unity is to the growth and health of their community (Loh 11). As we will see in Chapter 4, the conflict between two prominent women in Philippi—Evodia and Syntyche—caused a crisis that required Paul to call the Philippians back to unity for the sake of all the believers in Philippi.

5 because you have shared in proclaiming the Good News from the very first day until now.

When Paul first visited Philippi on his Second Missionary Journey (see Acts 16), he shared the message of the Good News of Messiah to Lydia and other women participating in Jewish prayer on Shabbat near the river. Lydia came to believe the message of Yeshua as Messiah and became the first believer in Philippi, and she then shared the message with her whole household, who became followers of Yeshua. Lydia and her family's early and enthusiastic response to the Good News of Yeshua set an example for the continued growth of the Philippian Community and their supportive efforts to spread the Good News.

From Lydia, the first believer in Philippi, the work of bringing the Good News to Philippi and beyond became a priority for the Philippian Messianic Community. Their work of spreading the Good News involved active and ongoing participation in the work of Paul (Loh 11), which continued from his first visit to now many years later. By their example they showed their commitment to Yeshua and followed the example of Paul, extending the work of his ministry, even while he was in chains in Rome.

The close relationship between Paul and the Philippians, demonstrated in these opening greetings, is also shown in their actions of sharing the Good News about Yeshua. The love that Paul has for the Philippians and that the Philippians have for Paul comes from their love for Yeshua, leading them to their shared mission grounded in the Good News in which they believe and proclaim (Merida 24–25).

---

6 And I am sure of this: that the One who began a good work among you will keep it growing until it is completed on the Day of the Messiah Yeshua.

Paul attested to the faithfulness of the Philippians will continue to grow until the Messiah's return, at which time they will see the fullness of their salvation and resurrection to eternal life in the presence of God and Messiah Yeshua. Paul also shares his expectancy that Yeshua will return soon (Loh 13) and uses this sense of expectation as an extra level of assurance to the believers in Philippi, especially for those like him facing persecution for their faith.

Paul's confidence is rooted in his trust in God's faithfulness to bring redemption and his firm conviction that Yeshua is the source of the redemption (Bockmuehl 61). Paul can, in confidence, confirm that through their excellent work, the Philippians will continue to grow in their faith and life of service to Yeshua. The fruit of their faith and life of service shows they are continuing to grow and become more like the Messiah; Paul, therefore, has confidence to assure them of their standing now and their future completion when Messiah returns (Merida 27).

"The Day of Messiah Yeshua" takes the "Day of the Lord" references to the One God of Israel and demonstrates the divine nature of Yeshua; the "Day of the Lord" and "The Day of Messiah Yeshua" become, in Paul's teaching, references to the lordship of Yeshua as the End Times judge of the created order (Keener 558).

7 It is right for me to think this way about you all, because I have you on my heart; for whether I am in chains or defending and establishing the Good News, you are all sharing with me in this privileged work.

Paul here speaks of his deep affection for the Philippians, who have been supportive of his work and have demonstrated their faithfulness to the Messiah. His love for them is grounded in their faithfulness and love for him expressed by them in their daily life. In his use of the word συγκοινωνός (*synkoinōnos*) for "sharing," Paul here commends the Philippians for their participation in doing outreach work based on his example. Also given that Paul was in prison, he appreciated the Philippians' continuing love and partnership as he awaits an impending capital trial before the Emperor (Hansen 53).

8 God can testify how I long for all of you with the deep affection of the Messiah Yeshua.

Paul here calls on God as his witness to his deep love for the Philippians. This act reflects ancient custom to invoke the name of a deity to back the integrity of your words (Keener 558). Paul had a deep love for the Messianic Community in Philippi. In verse 3 above, he shared with them, "I thank my God every time I think of you." His love for them was grounded in the Philippians' service and sacrifice for him.

Paul so identified his being in Messiah that here he can share with the Philippians that his love for them reflected the love Yeshua had for them, and through Paul, they know the love of the Messiah (Loh 15).

9 And this is my prayer: that your love may more and more overflow in fullness of knowledge and depth of discernment,

Paul here calls the Philippians to grow deeper in their love for one another and love of God and his Messiah so that they will grow in discernment and knowledge of the truth as they will need to stand against false teaching from within and without their community. Paul calls for them to overflow with wisdom and discernment so that they can stand against any distraction from the pagan world, including false teachers claiming to teach new truths outside the firm foundation that Paul had laid for them. Rather than focusing on health or financial gain as was common in pagan prayers, Paul demonstrated that his prayer was for the Philippians to grow in their knowledge of God and their daily walks serving Him (Thielman 349).

10 so that you will be able to determine what is best and thus be pure and without blame for the Day of the Messiah,

This call for building up discernment is essential to keep the Philippians on the right path without distraction as they strive for the Day of the Messiah and the Messianic Kingdom. In Philippi, there were many false teachings, but Paul calls on the Philippians to have the discernment to choose the best path, the godly path, so that they can stand blameless as they await the Day of the Messiah (Thielman 349). Paul urges them to wisely choose the best that God has for them to do and not to settle for a lesser way of living for God (Stern, *Commentary* 594). In short, they are to live blameless lives of purity.

11 filled with the fruit of righteousness that comes through Yeshua the Messiah—to the glory and praise of God.

All of their learning and communal life should lead to righteousness and right living that shows fruit, tangible demonstrations of the work of the Spirit of God in their lives. In Galatians 5:22a Paul gives examples of what the fruit of a righteous life should be: "...the fruit of the Spirit is love, joy, peace, patience, kindness, goodness, faithfulness, humility, self-control."

In bearing fruit with such values, Paul teaches them that they bring glory and praise to the God of Israel, thereby modeling the Messiah who brought glory to the Father as shown in Yeshua's "High Priestly Prayer" in Yochanan (John) 17:4: "I glorified you on earth by finishing the work you gave me to do."

Paul in Chains and the Spread of the Gospel (1:12–14)

12 Now, brothers, I want you to know that what has happened to me has helped in advancing the Good News.

Paul here addresses the Philippians as "brothers," the Greek word αδελφοι (*adelphoi*), which can more fully mean "brothers and sisters." In referring to the Philippians as his brothers and sisters, Paul is making clear to this mostly Gentile community of Yeshua followers that they, like Paul and the other Jewish Yeshua followers, are in the same spiritual family, united in their shared connection to the God of Israel by trusting in Yeshua as Messiah (Bockmuehl 73).

Paul now transitions to current news on himself and the work of ministry (Thielman 350). Though it may seem counter to what we would understand today, Paul shares that his imprisonment was an excellent opportunity for him to share the Gospel. Empowered by his faith in Yeshua, Paul looks beyond his own needs and sufferings to encourage the work of the Gospel.

13 It has become clear to the whole palace and to everyone else that it is because of the Messiah that I am in chains.

Paul's most significant source of empowering and encouragement is that the Good News of Yeshua is spreading and even influencing those in the Emperor's palace (Stern, *Commentary* 594). Paul's imprisonment brought the Good News of Yeshua to Rome, the heart of the Roman Empire. Paul brought a Jewish message to the heart of the pagan Roman world as R. Kent Hughes (48) stated when he wrote:

> They (the Romans) heard the astonishing story of the long-promised Jewish Messiah, who was crucified as the Jewish Scriptures predicted and was resurrected as their Scriptures predicted and, amazingly, forgives sins through his death and resurrection.

Paul made clear in Rome that the source of new life and life eternal was only available to both Jew and Gentile because of the work of the Jewish Messiah. Paul's call to Yeshua-faith included acceptance of the Jewish God, the Jewish Messiah, and the guidance of the Jewish Scriptures. For Jews this meant a continued life of faithfulness to *Torah* commands and for the

Gentile adherents the mysterious inclusion of them into the faith of Israel as Gentiles. Even those living in the imperial palace had heard about Paul's imprisonment, and there were those who came to trust in Yeshua. The word that there were believers in Yeshua in the Emperor's palace would serve to encourage the Philippians as they came to see that even among the elite of Roman society there were followers of Yeshua, a fact that could serve as encouragement in their faith (Thielman 351).

14 Also, my being in prison has given most of the brothers in the Lord confidence, so that they have become much more bold in speaking the word of God fearlessly.

Along with helping to make the message of Yeshua known throughout Rome, Paul's imprisonment for the Gospel also built up the faith of the Yeshua followers in Rome. Their confidence and boldness could inspire the believers in Philippi, who were also facing persecution and imprisonment, and Paul in this letter will champion willingness to suffer on behalf of faith in Yeshua, based on Yeshua's faithfulness in suffering (Bockmuehl 75).

Proclaiming the Messiah out of Jealousy (1:15–20)

15 True, some are proclaiming the Messiah out of jealousy and rivalry, but others are doing it in goodwill.

One of the critical themes of this letter is humility. This theme reaches a zenith in Philippians 2 where Paul gives us the example of Yeshua and the humility that led him to death on a

Roman execution stake. In verses 15 and 16, Paul contrasts those who share the Good News of the Messiah out of self-ambition and for their own fame with those who share the Good News humbly. Paul here is not criticizing their message but rather their spirit of self-ambition. Paul elaborates below in verse 18, where he commends that the word of Yeshua that is spreading even if done by unworthy messengers (Bockmuehl 78).

16 The latter act from love, aware that I am put where I am for defending the Good News; **17** while the former announce the Messiah out of selfish ambition, with impure motives, supposing they can stir up trouble for me in prison.

Some of the proclaimers of the Good News were doing it out of impure motives, such as self-aggrandizement and criticism of Paul.

18 But so what? All that matters is that in every way, whether honestly or in pretense, the Messiah is being proclaimed; and in that I rejoice. Yes, and I will continue to rejoice,

Paul here does not excuse those who share the Good News for impure motives but focuses on the sharing of the Good News. Where there is a false presentation of the Good News, Paul will speak out forcefully, but here the message is right though the presenter has wrong motives and Paul rejoices in the Good News being spread (Bockmuehl 81). Like other

Jewish teachers, Paul was willing to focus on the service performed for God, in this case, the sharing the Good News. Though the motives of presenters may be flawed, Paul was confident knowing that if the right message goes forth, lives will change for the better. (Keener 559). In short, Paul focuses on the content of the message, the Good News of Yeshua, which is perfect and leads to salvation and not the imperfect messenger (Stern *Commentary* 594) .

Paul knew that people were coming to know God and becoming followers of Yeshua through the word of truth., David H. Stern puts it this way:

> It is the Gospel that saves, not the preacher. The insincere evangelist is storing up for himself judgment, but those who have come to Yeshua because of his words have entered eternal life. (594)

---

19 for I know that this will work out for my deliverance, because of your prayers and the support I get from the Spirit of Yeshua the Messiah.

In this verse, Paul quotes the words of Job from Job 13:16a from the Septuagint, taking Job's words to defend himself, declare his faith in God's deliverance, and apply them to his own life and situation as a righteous sufferer (Das 5). As Job was an innocent victim of affliction and pain, Paul draws on the example of Job to parallel his affliction in serving Yeshua, and he takes comfort from the example of Job's eventual redemption from suffering and renewal of life (Bockmuehl 82).

20 It all accords with my earnest expectation and hope that I will have nothing to be ashamed of; but rather, now, as always, the Messiah will be honored by my body, whether it is alive or dead.

Paul wrote the Philippians this letter from prison where he was awaiting his appearance before the Roman Emperor Nero. As he faces the reality of his execution and impending death, Paul reflects on his life and his great desire that the Messiah will be honored now as he lives and that his death would also bring honor to Messiah and move forward the message of the Good News. As seen earlier in verses 12–14, Paul shares that the believers are receiving strength in their faith and people are coming to faith because of his imprisonment, and he looked forward to more good for the Kingdom coming from his imminent death for the Messiah.

Paul's understanding of the importance of living as well as possibly dying for the honor of God can be seen in the example of Rabbi Akiva (Berakhot 61B), who, while being killed by the Romans, understood that his death was the way he could finally "love God with all his soul" (Bockmuehl 86).

To Live or Die? (1:21–26)

21 For to me, life is the Messiah, and death is gain.

This verse is one of the more familiar verses from Paul's letters. Here we can see the heart of Paul and the extent of his transformation, which had begun with his Yeshua encounter on the road to Damascus in Acts 9:3–6. From that point onward, all of his life centered on the Messiah. All that he did was for and in Yeshua. Living itself for Paul was bound up with Yeshua. After encountering Yeshua, Paul could not conceive of life outside of his service to Messiah, and he seeks to teach the Philippians this vital truth—to truly live, one must be serving Yeshua (Loh 19). Paul understands that his life was now all about his connection to Yeshua and serving the Messiah as he explains in his letter to Galatia:

> When the Messiah was executed on the stake as a criminal, I was too; so that my proud ego no longer lives. But the Messiah lives in me, and the life I now live in my body I live by the same trusting faithfulness that the Son of God had, who loved me and gave himself up for me. (Gal. 2:20)

Paul's life was living for the Messiah and sharing the life-changing Good News about Yeshua with everyone he came in contact. Sharing the Good News was not an activity for Paul but his very reason for living. Serving God and serving others was his life work and his very reason for continuing to live. Emphasizing the full nature of Paul's life in Messiah, Charles Spurgeon (1598) expanded on this verse when he wrote:

> For to me to live is Christ—to know Christ more, to imitate Christ more, to preach Christ more, and to enjoy Christ more. And to die is gain.

Given the possibility, or more appropriately the probability, of execution awaiting him after his appearance before Nero, Paul also reflects on what death means to him. Living for Yeshua is his joy and passion, but if he dies, he will gain even more connection to Yeshua by entering into Messiah's presence to experience eternal life in Messiah. Though death could be an escape from the suffering of his life, to Paul death is not about his desire to end his suffering but gaining a closer connection to Yeshua (Bockmuehl 87).

Paul understood that Yeshua was the center and meaning of his life and his relationship with Yeshua meant suffering, which one day would end with his eternal union with the Messiah. Paul could be confident in his future free of suffering based on the example of Yeshua's suffering and exaltation as we will see in the Messianic hymn of Philippians 2. His confidence in the future was substantiated by his knowledge of the past events of Yeshua's life (Bockmuehl 83) .

22 But if by living on in the body I can do fruitful work, then I don't know which to choose.

Paul knows that death means immediate union with the Messiah in the eternity. He also realizes that continuing to live would allow him to continue to work for the Messiah here on earth, share the Gospel, and encourage the Messianic Community.

23 I am caught in a dilemma: my desire is to go off and be with the Messiah—that is better by far—

Paul encounters a dilemma: deciding between two outcomes that are equally good, one for himself—union with the Messiah—and the other for the Messianic Community—

his continued service to the body of believers. He continues his internal debate, recognizing that his death is the better choice because with the end of his race comes the reward of eternal spiritual connection to the Messiah.

24 but because of you, the greater need is to stay on in the body.

Leaving this world is by far better for Paul but he realized he still could do fruitful work sharing the Gospel and encouraging the believers in Rome and throughout the world through his letters, and if given release from prison, return to visit the Messianic communities of Asia Minor and Macedonia that he had established. Paul is teaching the Philippians an essential lesson in how they can emulate the Messiah by Paul's example of servanthood to them. Paul is demonstrating that the choice of service to others is more important than one's desires and therefore Paul knows that his decision is made for him to stay and serve the Messianic Community (Aymer, loc. 7549).

Paul knows that being united with the Messiah is his life's goal. But out of love and commitment to the Philippians, Paul was willing to delay the ultimate prize of faithfulness by instead modeling the Master and serving the Philippians (and others) as long as he can in this life, knowing that eternal life and union with the Messiah awaits him when his work on Earth is completed (Stern *Commentary* 594).

25 Yes, I am convinced of this; so I know I will stay on with you in order to help you progress in the faith and have joy in it.

After his short internal debate, Paul comes to his decision: to live and continue his work helping Yeshua followers grow in their faith. As a slave of the Messiah and a slave of the Messianic Community, Paul decides to put the work of his ministry ahead of his desire to leave this world and be united with Messiah in eternity. This decision is a true testimony of his heart to serve fellow and future believers as well as Yeshua.

---

26 Then, through my being with you again, you will have even greater reason for boasting about the Messiah Yeshua.

Paul here looks forward to physically returning to Philippi (and presumably the other Messianic communities) to personally teach and disciple believers to grow more mature in their Yeshua faith and walk. Paul spoke earlier of how lives were changed by his imprisonment (1:12–14), with the result that Yeshua followers were being strengthened in their faith through the witness of Paul's life and his willingness to suffer for Messiah. In this light, Moisés Silva (76) rendered the second half of this verse, "so that your boasting may abound in Christ Jesus through my ministry when I return to you." As with Paul's other teachings, the only source of proper boasting is in God and in Messiah Yeshua (see 1 Cor. 1:31 1 Cor. 3:21, and 2 Cor. 10:17). Paul essentially argues that his return to Philippi would demonstrate God's power, build up their faith, and give them a reason for boasting in God's ability to answer prayer (N.T. Wright *Everyone* 93).

Walking Worthy Lives (1:27-30)

27 Only conduct your lives in a way worthy of the Good News of the Messiah; so that whether I come and see you or I hear about you from a distance, you stand firm, united in spirit, fighting with one accord for the faith of the Good News,

Paul strongly encourages the Philippians to continue to live worthy lives that reflect their faith in the Good News they had received. Whether he returns to see them or hears about them, he calls them to live godly lives that are grounded in unity, a fundamental teaching of Paul.

Paul's call to unity in the lives of the Philippians reflects the corporate nature of faith. Though each person comes to trust in the Messiah as an individual, it is in a community—a unified body of believers—that individual and communal faith grows to be more like the Messiah. Moreover, the unity of the community would emulate the unity of Paul and the Messiah, demonstrating that the Philippians were following the way of the teacher, Paul, and their Master, Yeshua (Keown vol. 1 53–54).

In verse 27 the Greek word πολιτεύομαι (*politeuomai*), which Stern translated, "conduct your lives," is only used this one time in Paul's letters and only occurs one other time in the *B'rit Hadashah*—in Acts 23:1. In both references, the word refers to one's conduct as a citizen (Thielman 353). Paul's call to the Philippians is to help them understand their new way of life as not only followers of Yeshua but also citizens of Heaven and now to walk in the way of a heavenly citizen.

Interestingly, the Jewish historian Josephus used πολιτεύομαι (*politeuomai*) when describing how he "began to conduct" a Jewish way of life (which would have been based on *halakhah*, Jewish law and tradition):

> So when I had accomplished my desires, I returned back to the city, being now nineteen years old, and began to conduct myself according to the rules of the sect of the Pharisees, which is of kin to the sect of the Stoics, as the Greeks call them. (Life 2 12)

As Josephus chose to "conduct his life" in accordance with the *halakhic* way of life and practice of the Pharisees, Paul here is calling the Philippians to conduct their new lives as followers of Yeshua walking in the example of the Master (Hawthorne 69).

---

28 not frightened by anything the opposition does. This will be for them an indication that they are headed for destruction and you for deliverance. And this is from God;

The main 'opposition' to the Yeshua believers in Philippi would be from the pagan religions of their past and the syncretic religious observance of the city, including emperor worship. The Philippian Yeshua-followers had embraced a new Lord, Yeshua, (not an emperor), and faith in a crucified Jewish tradesman as their Messiah.

Paul here shows his confidence that the love and unity that is at the heart of the life of the Messianic Community in Philippi will enable them to stand firm in all circumstances, whether persecution by the Roman authorities, pagan religions, false teachers, and others that would come to persecute the community and break their unity. Their lives of unity, grounded in love and faith in Yeshua, will serve as a testimony to the opposition (whose lives lead to destruction). In contrast, the Philippians can look forward to deliverance. Paul's confidence of deliverance is built on the *Tanakh*'s promises of God's eventual vindication of his People (Keener 560).

29 because for the Messiah's sake it has been granted to you not only to trust in him but also to suffer on his behalf,

Though seemingly counterintuitive for suffering to be 'granted,'—a gift that the followers of Yeshua possess—Paul sees it as a privilege for himself to suffer on behalf of the Messiah and recommends the same attitude to the Philippians (Keener 560). This willingness to suffer for the Messiah can be seen in Acts 5:41 where we read:

> The emissaries left the Sanhedrin overjoyed at having been considered worthy of suffering disgrace on account of him.

Paul also acknowledged that his commitment to Yeshua was so deep that he was willing to follow Messiah's path of suffering, including death by execution (Anders 244). Paul states clearly to the Philippians the high cost of knowing Messiah: a path of suffering and death to endure before experiencing union with Yeshua fully in eternity.

30 to fight the same battles you once saw me fight and now hear that I am still fighting.

As one who has faced much persecution, Paul calls the Philippians to follow his example —a road of suffering. As Paul has faced opposition to his faith in Yeshua and his proclamation of the Good News, he calls the believers in Philippi to stand firm and emulate his willingness to suffer for the faith.

Along with rejecting their familial religious heritage or syncretic pagan practices, they have chosen another way, a way of rejection with outsider status. Their Yeshua faith has placed them at odds with their earthly society and they now must be willing to bear the cost of following Yeshua.

PHILIPPIANS 2

and every tongue will acknowledge that Yeshua the Messiah is Adonai — to the glory of God the Father.
—Philippians 2:11

Chapter Introduction

In Chapter 2, Paul gives us a powerful, even poetic declaration of the eternal divine nature of Yeshua and his place as one with the One God of Israel. Many scholars understand that a full acceptance of Yeshua's divine nature and union with the One God of Israel, referred to as a "High Christology," was a development of the Nicene Council of the fourth century c.e. and later Church councils. Yet in the Messianic hymn of 2:5–11, Paul presents Yeshua as the divine Messiah, the One God of Israel becoming a human being, in a letter written around 65 c.e. This Messianic hymn clearly shows that Paul and the earliest Messianic Community proclaimed a "High Christology" almost 300 years before Nicaea.

Though the Christological implications of the "Messianic Hymn" is usually the focus of writing and teaching from this chapter, it is of note that in the wider scope of the letter, Paul here is primarily focusing on the teaching the humility of the Messiah as an example to the Philippians. Yeshua's divine nature and his emptying of himself to become a man is seen here as emphasizing the profound nature of his humility in leaving his divine status to becoming part of the created order. This leads into Paul's important theme in Philippians his teaching on humility, in this chapter Paul presents the greatest example of humility, Messiah Yeshua (2:5–11), followed by examples of humble fellow believers the Philippians knew well: Timothy (2:19–24) and Epaphroditus (2:25–30).

Commentary

To Model the Messiah (2:1–4)

---

1 Therefore, if you have any encouragement for me
from your being in union with the Messiah, any comfort
flowing from love, any fellowship with me in the Spirit,
or any compassion and sympathy,
2 then complete my joy by having a common purpose and
a common love, by being one in heart and mind.
3 Do nothing out of rivalry or vanity; but, in humility,
regard each other as better than yourselves—

Paul encourages the Philippians to identify with and model Yeshua's character qualities, which will naturally stem from the Philippians' being in union with Yeshua and will reflect Yeshua's *humility*—one of the major themes of the letter and especially this chapter. Paul urges the Philippians to humbly value other believers as they not only model the Messiah but also grow beyond modeling to imitating the Messiah in daily life (Boa loc. 782).

In this call to unity as well as a call for the Philippians to bring Paul joy in the modeling of the Messiah, Paul encourages the Philippians to:

> Have the Same Mind (relates to encouragement/exhortation)
> Have the Same Love (relates to consolation—persuasiveness of Christ's love)
> Have the Same Soul (relates to partnership/fellowship of the Holy Spirit)
> Have the Same Goal (relates to affection and compassion)
> (Brown *Heavenly 3* 1–2).

As we will see below in the Messianic hymn of verses 5–11, this unified heart and mind reflects Yeshua's humble servanthood and self-sacrifice. Unity comes from humility and this is the way to model the Messiah and build up the Messianic Community.

---

4 look out for each other's interests and not just for your own.

Paul requests that the Philippians seek the best for others and not just themselves just as he himself continues demonstrating the self-sacrificing love and humble service of the Messiah. To be like the Messiah is to be other-centered and Messiah-centered (Boa loc. 782) and have the mindset of Yochanan the Immerser, who, speaking about Yeshua, declared: "He must become more important, while I become less important» (Yochanan/John 3:30).

The Messianic Hymn (2:5–11)

5 Let your attitude toward one another be governed by
your being in union with the Messiah Yeshua:
6 Though he was in the form of God,
he did not regard equality with God
something to be possessed by force.
7 On the contrary, he emptied himself,
in that he took the form of a slave
by becoming like human beings are.
And when he appeared as a human being,
8 he humbled himself still more
by becoming obedient even to death—
death on a stake as a criminal!
9 Therefore God raised him to the highest place
and gave him the name above every name;
10 that in honor of the name given Yeshua,
every knee will bow—
in heaven, on earth and under the earth—
11 and every tongue will acknowledge
that Yeshua the Messiah is Adonai —
to the glory of God the Father.

These verses represent a "Messianic hymn," which tells of the coming of the Messiah into the world as a "slave," his death on the Roman stake, and his exaltation to being Lord of all creation. Many scholars believe Paul was quoting from a previously written hymn or liturgical prayer that the people of Philippi would have believed and even used in their corporate worship as a teaching tool to emphasize the humility Yeshua perfectly modeled and Paul called them to pursue (Leman loc. 5). Larry Hurtado agrees that these verses can be understood to be an early Messianic Jewish hymn/liturgical prayer (*One God* 106), similar to other hymns in existence at the time of Paul's letter, which would have been familiar to the Philippian community. Hymns sung to a hero or a god were common at Greek religious festivals, so the new followers of Yeshua would be familiar with this genre and the use of hymns to honor Yeshua would be part of their understanding (Sanders *Apostle's* 602). The use of hymns and psalms in Temple or synagogue worship would have been familiar to Jewish Philippians.

James Waddell suggested that Paul's hymn originated from an earlier Aramaic liturgical prayer and that Paul translated it into Greek for inclusion here in his letter (190). Waddell argued for the pre-Pauline, Aramaic origins of the hymn:

> The conspicuous absence of definite articles, copulae, and other Greek particles typical of narrative prose, as well as the absence of an identifiable Greek meter, all are good evidence that Philippians 2:6–11 is a translation to Greek of what was originally an Aramaic hymn. (195)

Frank S. Thielman also advocated a pre-Pauline composition of the hymn:

> …these verses begin with the pronoun "who," possibly a clue that they are an excerpt from a larger composition. They also use several words that appear nowhere else in Paul's letters, and they seem to fall naturally into two balanced parts, verses 6-8 describing Christ's humiliation and verses 9-11 his exaltation (355).

Gordon Fee, however, understood the hymn to be Pauline in origin:

> In fact, it is a thoroughly Pauline sentence, with Pauline idioms, Pauline use of the Septuagint, Pauline theology, and the basic Pauline confession that the Lord is none other than Jesus Christ. (*Christology* 395)

Markus Bockmuehl also understood Philippians 2:5–11 as being Pauline, representing a poetic flow from verses 1 to 4 that leads into the hymn based on the shared language and theology (104). Adding to the discussion of whether the hymn was a previously available hymn that Paul used in his letter or whether it was a Pauline creation, Matthew Novenson asserted: "Pre-Pauline traditions, once used by Paul, become functionally Pauline and must be interpreted as meaningful parts of the texts in which they fall" (370 n. 56).

As the prayers of the *siddur* (Jewish prayer book) express Jewish theological concepts and development, this liturgical hymn gives us an early look at the evolution of Messianic Jewish theology and early liturgical development within the growing Messianic Jewish and Messianic Gentile communities (Couch Phil. 2:5). The construction of liturgical prayers and hymns like this one, which took Isaiah 45:23, a passage from the *Tanakh* that applied to the One God of Israel, and referred it to Yeshua showed an early understanding of the divine nature of Yeshua by the earliest of Yeshua followers. We can also see in this liturgical development an early theological understanding of first-century Messianic Jews that the nature of the God of Israel is more complicated than a strict monotheism (Hurtado *One God* 133). In Yeshua, the divine nature is shared and yet is within the framework of One God.

Though two millennia of theologians would wrestle with the place of Yeshua as well as the *Ruach HaKodesh* (Holy Spirit) within the One God of Israel expressed in the *Shema* (the core Jewish prayer from Deut. 6:4), it appears that the earliest Yeshua followers accepted that the God of Israel became a human being in Yeshua. In line with the liturgical use of the Psalms in their worship, the early followers created liturgical songs honoring Yeshua as Messiah and Lord that were used in worship meetings and private devotionals (Shillington 221).

In addition to containing one of the most potent and straightforward teachings on the eternal divine nature of Yeshua, the hymn also teaches the Philippians essential lessons of humility modeled on the Messiah's humility and servanthood (Dobson 1508). Such servanthood and self-sacrifice offered a way for the Philippians to model the kind of unity Paul laid out in the first four verses of the chapter (Waddell 191). Let's look more closely at the hymn, line by line.

---

5 Let your attitude toward one another be governed by your being in union with the Messiah Yeshua:

Paul here called the Philippians to take on a communal attitude of unity that reflected "being in union [unity] with Messiah Yeshua" as the starting point. From this union comes one of the essential lessons of Philippians: unity, especially unity through humility within the Messianic Community. With Yeshua as the ultimate example of humility as seen in the Messianic hymn, Paul calls all the Philippians to embrace the humble example of Yeshua in their lives to bring unity.

As the community as a whole begins to embrace humility, then there is true unity and an end to strife and dissension (Spurgeon 1599).

For "union with the Messiah" to be genuine requires a life that imitates and models that of the Messiah. In walking with his humility and self-sacrifice, the followers of Yeshua can fully live out the Messiah's example; more than being just "followers" or "believers," they become living witnesses of the Messiah. Those that model this way of living become the "good news of Messiah" in our world and model Messiah and walk in his ways (Bates 204).

---

6 Though he was in the form of God, he did not regard equality with God something to be possessed by force.

In this verse we see Paul beginning his teaching on Yeshua's emergence into the world as a humble servant, the highest example of humility that Paul addresses in this letter. In speaking of Yeshua in the "form of God," Craig Keener (560) has noted that some scholars see a contrast between Adam, who was created in God's image (Gen. 1:26) as a human that sought divine knowledge and status by eating the forbidden fruit in Eden (Gen. 3:5), and Yeshua, who was eternally divine and came into our world humbly as a human.

Novation, a third-century c.e. Christian theologian cited in the *Ancient Christian Commentary on Scripture*, wrote:

> If Christ were only a man, he would have been said to have been "in the image of God," not "in the form of God." We know that humanity was made in the image, not the form, of God. (Edwards Phil. 2:6a)

Yeshua's pre-incarnation status was and remained divine "in the form of God." As fully divine Yeshua became a man in contrast to his being just a human "in the image of God" on a divine mission.

In keeping with the letter's theme of humility, Yeshua set aside his place in glory to come into the world as the greatest example of humility, going from the height of divinity to becoming a human—and as we will see in verse 7, assuming the lowest form of human, a slave who will be executed on the Roman stake. As the divine Son, Yeshua came into our world as a slave, on a singular mission to bring redemption to the world by his death on the stake, demonstrating the highest level of humility by willingly giving himself to service on behalf of those he came to seek and save. Although as Messiah he had full rights to all that is divine in his incarnation, he did not seize this power (nor "possessed [it] by force") but he willingly died as a man without exploiting his divine nature.

The pre-existence of a divine Messiah was an established belief in Judaism, seen in the *Tanakh*, most notably in the Servant Songs of Isaiah especially Isaiah 52:13–53:12 (Stern *Commentary* 596). In the Talmud, we also see that the pre-existence of the Messiah was part of early Rabbinic thought. In b. Pesahim 54A we read:

> …Seven things were created before the world was made, and these are they: Torah, repentance, the Garden of Eden, Gehenna, the throne of glory, the house of the sanctuary, and the name of the Messiah….And the name of the Messiah: "His name shall endure forever and has existed before the sun." (Ps. 72:17) (Neusner, b. Pesahim 54A).

The rabbis listed seven things that pre-existed the creation of the world, the seventh being the name of the Messiah, which came from Psalm 72:17, which reads in full:

> May his name endure forever, his name, Yinnon, as long as the sun. May people bless themselves in him, may all nations call him happy.

In Verse 6, Paul speaks plainly and without explanation about the pre-existence of Yeshua in line with established Jewish thought concerning the pre-existence of the Messiah, and much like the opening of Genesis 1, where God is presented as the Creator of all things. Here Paul makes clear his deep understanding and core theological belief that Yeshua is the pre-existent Son of God who was the source of the Creation of the world.

We can see Paul speaking of the pre-existence of Yeshua as the source of the creation of the cosmos (Oden 53) in his correspondence with the Messianic community in Corinth where he wrote:

> yet for us there is one God, the Father, from whom all things come and for whom we exist; and one Lord, Yeshua the Messiah, through whom were created all things and through whom we have our being. (1 Corinthians 8:6)

As was seen in the Talmud (b. Pesahim 54A), Paul here places Yeshua the Messiah into the creation of the cosmos. The One who entered humbly into our world as part of creation was the One who was the source of all creation.

The Jewish traditions related to Enoch demonstrate that the belief in a divine Messianic figure was understood and part of Jewish understanding and expectations (Boyarin 76). In 1 Enoch 37–71 we see the Hebrew word מָשִׁיחַ (mashiach) twice in reference to a Heavenly transcendent figure (Neusner, Aver-Peck & Green Vol. 2, p. 878). In this, we can see that the eternal nature of the Messiah was a well-understood belief among the early Yeshua followers in Philippi and elsewhere (Mackintosh 66).

Paul here puts forth what is known as a "high Christology," an understanding of the eternal divine nature of Yeshua that he bore even before his birth into our world (Fredriksen, *Pagans* 144). An early high Christology within the earliest Messianic Community, argues Daniel Boyarin (52–53), can be seen from the belief in the divine Messiah, the Messiah as God-man based in Jewish tradition grounded in the prophecies of Daniel. Boyarin further attests:

> I submit that it is possible to understand the Gospel only if both Jesus and the Jews around him held to a high Christology whereby the claim to Messiahship was also a claim to being a divine man. Were it not the case, we would be very hard-pressed to understand the extremely hostile reaction to Jesus on the part of Jewish leaders who did not accept his claim (55).

Though scholars debate the early nature of the belief in the eternal divine nature of Yeshua among his earliest followers and credit it to later development at the Council of Nicea, we can see here that Paul, writing in the 60s of the Common Era, clearly puts forward a divine Yeshua, who, like the Father, was pre-existent before the incarnation (Sanders, *Apostle's* 603).

We can also see a reference to Yeshua as the second Adam in this verse. As the first Adam chose to eat the forbidden fruit that would make him "like God, knowing good and evil" (Gen. 3:5b), Yeshua as the second Adam, in contrast, chose to lay aside his place as God to come into this world to live as a man (Waddell 149).

The second half of the verse teaches the eternal power and glory of godhood that Yeshua willingly set aside for his life on Earth:

> Philippians 2:6 must be understood to mean that Christ's "equality with God" was not something he exploited; that is, such equality was intrinsically his, but so great was his humility and subservience to the will of his Father that he chose not to exploit it but took the path of humiliation, incarnation, and death on a cross (Carson 501).

---

7 On the contrary, he emptied himself, in that he took the form of a slave by becoming like human beings are. And when he appeared as a human being,

---

The Greek word for "emptied" is κενόω (*kenoō*). Many scholars understand that Yeshua, in his incarnation, emptied himself of the omnipotence, omnipresence, and omniscience of God (Stern, *Commentary* 597). Emptying could signify the sinless Savior's sacrificial death, where he poured out his life and bore the sins of many (Dobson 1510).

In this verse, Paul teaches that Yeshua the eternal Messiah came into the world as a flesh-and-blood human being, in contrast to later Gnostic groups and the proto-Gnostic teachings of the time, which espoused that the man Yeshua *became* divine or the divine Yeshua just *appeared* to be in the world (Lockyer 30).

As Yeshua, God became man and entered into his creation uniquely and intimately. While there had been brief glimpses of the One God of Israel in the *Tanakh* interacting with human beings, in the *B'rit Hadashah* (New Testament) scriptures Yeshua as the One God of Israel empties himself to enter the world fully and encounter his created beings as one of them (O'Callaghan 14). As Paul models Yeshua in his life and calls the Philippians to join him in becoming more and more in Messiah, Paul shares the example of Yeshua's lowly entry into our world and his life of submission to the divine plan as the model for the Philippians to emulate.

He took the form of a slave

More than just becoming a human being, however, Yeshua became a slave. Paul shows the example of Yeshua's willingness to be a "slave" as one accepting the lowest place in society. Interestingly, in the opening of the letter (Philippians 1:1), Paul makes the Philippians aware that both he and Timothy as "slaves" are modeling the humility and submission to Messiah Yeshua that they are calling the believers in Philippi to pursue with them (Hanson 209). As "slaves of the Messiah Yeshua," Paul and Timothy model their devotion to the Messiah, just as Yeshua exemplified his devotion to us.

In both Philippians 1:1 and 2:7, Paul used a form of the Greek word δοῦλος (*doulos*), which Stern translates as "slave." *Doulos* can also be translated as "servant" or "bondservant." (Some Bibles including the ESV, use "servant" in these verses instead of "slave" but these terms are basically interchangeable because most "servants" were, in fact, "slaves" during this historical period). In the shared use of *doulos* for Paul and Timothy as well as Yeshua, we see a parallel between Paul and Timothy's devotion to Yeshua as his "slaves" and Yeshua as the "slave" of the divine plan leading to the Roman execution stake and his death as a slave to that plan.

In Isaiah 52:13, the beginning of the Servant Songs (which include Isaiah 53), we see the use of the Hebrew word עֶבֶד (*eved*) can be rendered "slave" or "servant" in English. Since the Greek word *doulos* was used in the Septuagint (LXX) to translate the Hebrew word *eved*, Paul could be making a connection between the Servant of Isaiah and Yeshua the Messiah.

In his humble entry into our world Yeshua became the embodiment of the Messianic aspirations seen in Isaiah's Servant Songs where we read: "even more he "exposed himself to death and … bearing the sin of many and interceding for the offenders" (Isa. 53:12).

In this verse we see the Messianic "servant/slave" laying down his life as an act of dying an atoning death just as Yeshua the Messiah would do.

Yeshua is the fulfillment of Isaiah's Servant Songs, of which Isaiah 53 is the best-known and most-often-quoted passage. Yeshua's humble entry into our world was more than just the One God of Israel entering the world as a man to live among and fellowship with his creation; Yeshua came into the world as a lowly slave/servant, demonstrating humility as he temporarily left the highest eternal state to assume the lowest earthly state.

Becoming like human beings are

There are two words in Greek, γίνομαι (*ginomai*) and γεννάω (*gennaō*), that can mean "born" or "become." In this verse, Paul used the Greek word *ginomai* rather than *gennaō* to convey the meaning of a change in status, which is what we see in Yeshua's emptying himself, temporarily leaving his pre-existent divine state and coming into our world as a human being (Bates 40). Other uses of *ginomai* in the *B'rit Hadashah* include the Transfiguration of Yeshua in Matthew 17:2: "As they watched, he began to *change form*—his face shone like the sun, and his clothing *became* as white as light" (emphasis added). In Matthew, *ginomai* is used to describe Yeshua's clothing changing to bright white as he makes his glory known to his closest *talmidim* (disciples). Through the Transfiguration, we can see the coming together of the human and divine in Yeshua. As Albert Nolan writes:

> Jesus' divinity is not something totally different from His humanity. Jesus' divinity is the transcendent depth of His humanity. Jesus was immeasurably more human than other men." (135)

Becoming a man was not a sign that Yeshua was inferior to the Father because his innate divine status, though humbled in the incarnation, demonstrated that "The obedience of Christ is the voluntary, joyful, thankful obedience of a Son—the true sacrificed, transparent obedience of an equal" (O'Callaghan 49).

In this act of humility, Yeshua as divine Lord entered into the world to seek and save, doing the work only God can do. Thus, the One God of Israel again steps into human history to offer redemption, which only comes from the "Divine One"

(Berlin 388). The role of Redeemer can only be filled by the One God of Israel:

> For *ADONAI* your God is God of gods and Lord of lords, the great, mighty and awesome God, who.:. secures justice for the orphan and the widow;…loves the foreigner, giving him food and clothing. (Deut. 10:17–18)

---

7 …And when he appeared as a human being, **8** he humbled himself still more by becoming obedient even to death—death on a stake as a criminal!

Yeshua's humility led to the execution stake (the cross), the sacrifice out of his love for the Father (Grenz 490). Yeshua's ultimate act of humility and obedience to the divine plan was his self-sacrifice at the stake. N.T. Wright summarizes the extent of Yeshua's humility and obedience:

> Though Christ's 'act of obedience' clearly refers to his death, in particular, the scope of Philippians 2:5–11 shows that it is wider, including the obedient and humble life which culminated on the cross. (*History* 74).

In the Messianic Hymn we see the dual nature of Yeshua that begins in his divine state and then he humbly enters the world as a slave that would die on the Roman stake and after his suffering would receive the Divine Name and be highly exalted. This dual role held by Yeshua unites the two major pictures of the Messiah, the Messiah ben David, the kingly "end of the ages" ruler and the Messiah ben Yosef, the "suffering servant" of Isaiah's servant songs, most notably Isaiah 53.

The dual nature of Yeshua as the Davidic Messiah as the divine royal king and also the Suffering Messiah that would give his life in an atoning sacrifice can be seen in the Midrash Rabbah, Ruth 5:6 that reads:

> … it refer[s] to the Messiah. COME HITHER: approach to royal state. AND EAT OF THE BREAD refers to the bread of royalty; AND DIP THY MORSEL IN THE VINEGAR refers to his sufferings, as it is said, But he was wounded because of our transgressions (Huckel Isa. 53:5).

In an unusual and even mystic way Yeshua in his atoning death on the Roman stake served as both the sacrifice and the priest offering the sacrifice as we see in the Letter to the Messianic Jews/Hebrews:

> But when the Messiah appeared as cohen gadol of the good things that are happening already, then, through the greater and more perfect Tent which is not man-made (that is, it is not of this created world), he entered the Holiest Place once and for all. And he entered not by means of the blood of goats and calves, but by means of his own blood, thus setting people free forever. For if sprinkling ceremonially unclean persons with the blood of goats and bulls and the ashes of a heifer restores their outward purity; then how much more the blood of the Messiah, who, through the eternal Spirit, offered himself to God as a sacrifice without blemish, will purify our conscience from works that lead to death, so that we can serve the living God!" (Hebrews 9:11–14)

This unique priestly role that Yeshua performed also can be seen in the two Messiahs of the Qumran community, the Davidic Messiah, common in Jewish Messianic expectations but also a Priestly Messiah (Neusner *Encyclopedia* Vol. 2 878). Though as we will see in Yeshua in contrast to the two Messiahs of Qumran, Yeshua will embody both the Priestly Messiah and the Davidic Messiah in his two comings, first as the priestly to redeem and the second to eternally rule and reign. As we see in Hebrews, Yeshua also played the role as the divinely ordained sacrificial lamb that Paul would speak about in his letter to Corinth (1 Cor. 5:7).

Paul is making the Philippians aware of the possible cost of obedience in modeling the humility of Yeshua. For followers of Yeshua and modelers of the Master, there is what Bonhoeffer called, "the cost of discipleship." The cost of following Yeshua can be seen earlier in the book when Paul said, "because for the Messiah's sake it has been granted to you not only to trust in him but also to suffer on his behalf" (Phil. 1:29). Paul also wanted the Philippians to understand that Yeshua, their Lord and Master, died the most humiliating death on their behalf. As E. P. Sanders wrote: "Christ did not just humble himself (becoming meek and mild), he degraded himself, going as low as death by crucifixion—the penalty meted out to rebellious slaves" (*Apostle's* 599).

Crucifixion was most problematic for Greeks and Romans to understand that the Lord of the Universe would be willing to die the worst death, the most humiliating death on their behalf, a punishment reserved for criminals who were not Roman citizens, a penalty for the lowest of criminals (Stern *Commentary* 597). This deep level of commitment to humility that Paul is calling the Philippians to understand and pursue is the way modeled by their Master (Dobson 1510). As the greatest act of humility, the Messiah's death is to be the point of unity for all followers of Yeshua. Paul is taking the Philippians to the Messiah's death on the Roman stake as the place where they can fully connect to the Messiah and understand their calling to emulate his humility, a humility that can and may lead to death for them (Spurgeon 1599).

---

9 Therefore God raised him to the highest place and gave him the name above every name;

Raised him to the highest place

In this verse, Paul used the Greek word ὑπερύψωσεν (*hyperypsōsen*), which means "super-exalted" or "hyper-exalted" (Sanders *Apostle's* 603). Paul here was showing that after his life and death as a slave on Earth, Yeshua did not just return to his previous place of exaltation in Heaven as the divine Son, but he returned to a higher level of exaltation, to the place of lordship over the whole created order as will be seen in verse 10 (Bates 40). Yeshua, who had been "super-degraded," would become the one who is "super-exalted." As the "Messianic hymn" seeks to teach Yeshua-like humility, it demonstrates that the exaltation of Yeshua was the outcome of his great acts of humility, especially his self-sacrificial death on the Roman stake (Giglio loc. 89669).

In Targum Jonathan on Isaiah 53:10, we see the exaltation and rewarding with the spoils of the Nations given to the

Messiah because of his willingness to suffer death on behalf of the divine plan and for the forgiveness of sins when we read:

> Then I will apportion unto him the spoil of great nations, and he shall divide as spoil the wealth of mighty cities, because he was ready to suffer martyrdom that the rebellious he might subjugate to the Torah. And he shall seek pardon for the sins of many and for his sake the rebellious shall be forgiven (Huckel Isa. 53:10).

It was this act of supreme humility that formed the basis from which Yeshua demonstrated his worthiness to exaltation to the highest place (Moltmann 106). Moreover, this exaltation represents the highest place of authority, which reflects Daniel's prophecy of the End of Days in Daniel 7:13–14, wherein the Son of Man (Yeshua) is granted eternal, universal rulership by the "Ancient of Days" (God the Father) (Boyarin 39) .

The name above every name

In speaking of "the name above every name," David H. Stern commented:

> Since God himself transcends human limits, it is not surprising that his nature cannot be expressed fully by the normal use of language. The fact that God transcends human limitation means that he exceeds what language can convey about him. (*Commentary* 597)

Scholars debate what Paul meant by "the name above every name." Two possibilities prevail: the birth name, Yeshua, or the *Tetragrammaton,* the unspoken name of the One God of Israel.

Yeshua

The first possibility for Paul's "name above every name" points to the human name of the Messiah, "Yeshua." Though Yeshua was a popular name during the first century C.E. for many males, scholars who favor this name as the "name above every name" back their assertion by often citing the divine biblical message through the angel who had visited Yeshua's mother, Miriam, which we read about at Yeshua's *b'rit-milah* (circumcision) in Luke 2:21: "On the eighth day, when it was time for his *b'rit-milah*, he was given the name Yeshua, which is what the angel had called him before his conception."

C. F. D. Moule asserted that the name "Yeshua" is "the name above every name" because it was the human name the Messiah was known by in the Incarnation and the name he bore in his self-emptying and self-sacrifice. The formerly common human name "Yeshua" is now exalted like the risen Yeshua himself is now exalted (Moule 270). According to Moule, the common name Yeshua became exalted by being the name of the Messiah who suffered and died. The divine Yeshua who came into this world as a servant, through his sacrifice, turned this common name into one to which all creation will one day bow and acknowledge the lordship of the bearer.

We can see an expanded version of the above points in this progression:

God (verse 6); then, second, a Jesus who, without ceasing to be truly and fully God, became truly man (verse 7); furthermore, he experienced death and, in particular, a death of shame and rejection on a cross (verse 8). From beginning to end there was continuity of person, for it was

Jesus Christ (verse 5) who was in the form of God, just as, at the other end of the process, it was Jesus (verse 10) who received the name which is above every name (verse 9) and to whom every tongue will yet confess (verse 11). (Motyer 120)

Tetragrammaton (the Unspoken Name of the One God of Israel)

R. Kendall Soulen (287) suggested that in the Jewish context of Paul's writing, "the name above every name" was the "Tetragrammaton," the unspoken name of the One God of Israel. The Tetragrammaton comes from the Greek Τετραγράμματον, meaning "[consisting of] four letters"), יהוה in Hebrew and YHWH in Latin script; it is the four-letter biblical name of the One God of Israel. Such a view upholds the highest form of Christology, declaring Yeshua›s place within the One God of Israel consistent with the *Tanakh*:

> Paul identifies the first person of the Trinity as the one who gives the Divine Name, the second person as the one who receives it, and the third person as the one who awakens its acknowledgment and glorification. (While the text does not explicitly mention the Holy Spirit, the Spirit's activity is implied by the universal acclamation of Jesus as "Lord," which Paul elsewhere says is possible only as a work of the Spirit). (1 Cor. 12:3) (Soulen 288)

As we will see in verses 10 and 11, the bearer of the "name above every name," Yeshua the Messiah, will receive universal acknowledgment and worship as the sovereign ruler of all Creation. For a Jew such as Paul this universal worship would belong only to the One God of Israel who is the sole one worthy to bear the Tetragrammaton/the Unspoken Name of the One God of Israel; therefore, we see that this "name above every name" must be the Divine Name (Tabletalk 40).

N.T. Wright saw a definite connection between Yeshua as Messiah also being *Kyrios*. Coming from the ancient Greek word κύριος, Kyrios (or Kurios) means "lord" or "master," appears about 740 times in the *B'rit Hadashah*, and usually refers to Yeshua. In addition, Wright asserted Yeshua's direct reference to the One God of Israel:

> … in Philippians 2:6–11—if Jesus has now been exalted to share the very throne of God, the God who (as Isaiah 45:23 declares) will not share his glory with another, then this Jesus must have been from all eternity, somehow or other, 'equal with God.' (*Resurrection* 395)

---

10 that in honor of the name given Yeshua, every knee will bow—in heaven, on earth and under the earth— **11** and every tongue will acknowledge that Yeshua the Messiah is Adonai—to the glory of God the Father.

Every knee will bow…every tongue will acknowledge.

In verses 10 and 11, we can see an application of Isaiah 45:23; for context let's look at verses 22–25:

> Look to me, and be saved, all the ends of the earth! For I am God; there is no other. In the name of myself I have sworn, from my mouth has rightly gone out, a word that will not return—that to me every knee will bow, and

> every tongue will swear about me that only in *Adonai* are
> justice and strength. All who rage against him will come
> to him ashamed, but all the descendants of Isra'el will
> find justice and glory in *Adonai* .

The passage from Isaiah 45 is a monotheistic passage where the One God of Israel is speaking of his rulership over all (C. Wright 262). Paul applied this passage to Yeshua as an acknowledgment of the lordship of the Messiah (Friesen 282). Paul is expressly teaching the divine nature of the Messiah, and given Paul's belief in the unity of the God of Israel grounded in the *Shema*, this belief has been called "binitarian monotheism" (Hurtado *How* 51). Paul is expressing his understanding of Yeshua in union with the God of Israel (Leman loc. 9).

Given that Isaiah 45 clearly is about the One God of Israel, Paul's use of Isaiah's language in the hymn referring to Yeshua makes clear that Yeshua bears the place of cosmic Lord in union with the Father. Whereas the Greek word κυριος (*kurios*) can be just a title of respect for a human, such as "sir," the implication here is that Paul is making clear that Yeshua is the One God of Israel who became part of the created order (Stern *Commentary* 597).

In the words "every knee will bow—in heaven, on earth and under the earth," we see an expansion of the rulership of Yeshua beyond Israel and the nations but to a universal cosmic scale where Yeshua's reign and rulership includes the complete created order and the unseen spiritual world of the heavens and underworld (Boccaccini 127).

That there are gods or spiritual powers throughout the created order may seem foreign to modern readers but would have been commonplace for those reading the letter in Philippi where:

> Greeks worshiped gods in the heavens, earth, sea, and underworld; traditional Greek mythology also placed the shadowy existence of departed souls in the underworld. Paul announces that whatever categories of beings there are, they must acknowledge Christ's rule, because he is exalted above them. One often bowed the knee in obeisance before a ruler or deity. (Keener 561)

According to *The Complete Jewish Study Bible*, the three locations of "heaven, earth, and under the earth" refer to the angelic, human, and demonic realms, respectively (1690).

As we see in the command "to have no other gods" (Exod. 20:3) as an acknowledgment of the sole place of worship to be given to the One God of Israel, Paul radically teaches that Yeshua stands within Israel's monotheistic faith and shares in the divine worship that belongs only to the One God of Israel. Speaking as an observant Jew who is cognizant that worship is reserved only for the One God of Israel (as seen in multiple references in the *Tanakh*—for example: Exod. 20:3 5; Deut. 5:7 6:13 7:16 8:19 10:12 11:13; Josh. 24:14–16 20–21; 2 Kings 17:35; and Isa. 43:10 45:21 22 46:9), Paul nevertheless makes a clear assertion of Yeshua's divine status by referring to "every knee bowing" to Yeshua at the End of Days (Schreiner *Hebrews* 448).

Though it is Yeshua who receives the End of Days acknowledgment of lordship, it is still to the glory of God the Father. There is a sense of subordination of Yeshua to the Father, though it is also clear that this subordination does not preclude the understanding that Paul holds to the unity and equality of Yeshua with the Father (Stuckenbruck 131).

Ultimately, all of the created order will acknowledge the lordship of Yeshua—both Yeshua followers, who bend the knee with great joy and worship King Messiah, as well as non-followers, who will bow in acknowledgment of Yeshua's place as King of Kings and Lord of Lords. Some with joy and some with sadness but Yeshua will be recognized as Lord by all of creation, seen and unseen (Boring 226).

Both the seen and unseen opponents of Yeshua and his followers will know and acknowledge Yeshua and vindicate the faith of followers who have faced persecutions from these opponents. As all knees bow at the Name given to Yeshua, the full acknowledgment of the lordship of Yeshua over all creation will be clear (Fredriksen *Pagans* 140). Fredriksen (*Question* 199) saw in this verse that the whole created order, even the dark cosmic powers, bending the knee represent their turn to God and Yeshua at the End of Days. We can see a contrast to this understanding in the verses from Isaiah 45, which state that although all will bow, it is only the faithful who stand justified, while the others are shamed

This exaltation of Yeshua and universal bowing of the knees by the whole of the created order are directly related to Yeshua being faithful to the divine plan. Because of Yeshua's profound act of humility, accepting death on the Roman stake, all of the created order will bow to him and acknowledge him as King of Kings and Lord of Lords (Giglio loc. 89684).

Through this faithfulness of Yeshua leading to his universal acknowledgment of lordship, Paul unites the Suffering Servant of Isaiah 52:13–53:12 and the bowing of knees before the One

God of Israel in Isaiah 45:23 in the person of Yeshua according to James Ware:

> The Christ hymn thus reflects a connected reading of the latter part of Isaiah, in which the eschatological reign of God over the nations envisaged in Isaiah 45:18–25 is understood as the outcome of the suffering and exaltation of the Servant in Isaiah 52:13–53:12, identified with the crucified, risen and glorified Jesus Christ. (229)

Yeshua the Messiah is ADONAI

It is in verse 11 that we see the prophetic word about a coming day when all the created order acknowledges the messiahship and universal lordship of Yeshua. Paul stresses the critical place that Yeshua plays as the one to whom the Philippians were to focus their worship. In the context of Jewish monotheistic faith, there was only One God to whom reverence was due, and this was the One God of Israel made manifest to Abraham and his descendants.

The Greek word κυριος (*kurios* or *kyrios*), meaning "lord," which Stern translated as *ADONAI,* is used over six thousand times in the Septuagint (LXX) to translate the Tetragrammaton, the unspoken four-letter name of the One God of Israel, usually written in Latin characters as YHWH or YHVH (Oden 53). The use of the substitute name, *kurios* in Greek or אדֹנָי (*ADONAI*) in Hebrew is based on Jewish tradition and practice grounded in the Talmud (Pesachim 50a), which prohibited the pronunciation of the Divine Name as written in Hebrew (Stern *Commentary* 4).

Paul's use of *kurios* in this passage for Yeshua is an affirmation of his deity in that the most widely used title for the One God of Israel in the Septuagint is now being applied to Yeshua (Tabletalk 40). Here Paul unites Yeshua with the One God of Israel by declaring that Yeshua is *Adonai*. Yeshua is worthy of this worship because of his place as the bearer of the Divine Name and his position as Lord (C. Wright 260). It is as Lord and the One God of Israel that Yeshua is due worship and as the proper focus of prayer, especially in the context of Paul's monotheism grounded in the *Shema* (Robertson Phil. 2:11).

In using *kurios* to refer to Yeshua, Paul demonstrates what Paula Fredriksen called "radical" binitarianism (*Pagans* 144), a re-imagining of Jewish monotheism that allowed for the One God of Israel to include both the Father and Yeshua, the divine Son. This re-imaging of the oneness of the God of Israel highlights that at the core of Jewish monotheism is the devotion to one God (Kärkkäinen 14). Paul teaches that the Father and now Yeshua are bearers of the Divine Name, showing that there is only One God as they share the one Divine Name of the God of Israel.

In his three-volume *Systematic Theology*, Wolfhart Pannenberg wrote about how Yeshua finds his place in Jewish monotheism:

The title Kyrios implies the full deity of the Son. In the confession of Thomas in John 20:28 the titles God and Lord are expressly set alongside one another. Yet the Son is not Kyrios in competition with the Father but in honor of the Father (Phil 2:11). The confession of Jesus Christ as the one and only Kyrios in no way weakens the confession of the one God. The former confession is so related to the latter that all things proceed from the one God, the Father, but all are mediated through the one Kyrios (1 Cor 8:6) (vol. 1 266).

As the bearer of the Divine Name, Yeshua takes his place as sovereign over the created universe as the One to whom all knees bow (as seen in verse 10) and vow allegiance. The importance of Paul referring to Yeshua as Lord is making clear his place as the One ruler of all:

> That Jesus is Lord means that all alternative pretensions to power are finally reduced to nothingness (Oden 53).

Yeshua as bearer of the name of the One God of Israel is not just a god or a lord, he as the bearer of the divine name reduces all other authorities whether the gods of the Nations or any worldly rulers to nothingness. In this affirmation Yeshua is the sole ruler of the cosmos and the only one that is worthy to receive worship and the bending of the knees. Either voluntarily for followers of Yeshua or involuntarily for those who were not followers of Yeshua, either way, it will be Yeshua, the Messiah of Israel that the whole created order worships as Lord of Lords (κυριος κυριων), the one due allegiance, reverence, and adoration (Sproul 57). Not only is Yeshua declared as deity, the One God of Israel that came into the world, Yeshua is also acknowledged as the sovereign ruler of all; he is the sole God who is Lord of All to whom all of the created order owes allegiance (Brown *Heavenly 4* 10).

Not only is Paul making a profound religious declaration, acknowledging Yeshua the Messiah as bearing the Name of the One God of Israel, an especially profound statement for an observant Jew, but in light of the Roman world of his time, Paul here makes an intense and dangerous political statement: Yeshua is Lord and not Nero. Paul here contrasted his call to allegiance of the true Lord (Yeshua) in contrast to the expected allegiance to the false lord (Nero) and emphasized to the Philippians the cost of their faith in Yeshua (Pearson 219). The declaration of Yeshua's lordship was a statement in direct defiance to the emperor cult and the honor due to Nero as the Roman emperor (Taylor 26).

What is easily lost in focusing on Yeshua's exaltation and worship as cosmic Lord is the acknowledgment of his place as the Jewish Messiah. Much of Christian theology focuses solely on Yeshua as the cosmic Lord of the universe and Savior of the now multi-national People of God with recognition of his role as the Jewish Messiah and Savior of the Jewish People mainly relegated to apologetic and evangelistic purposes, for example, citing Yeshua as the culmination and fulfillment of the *Tanakh's* (Old Testament's) Messianic prophecies. Sometimes Yeshua is stripped of his Jewish connection altogether. But Yeshua's place as the Jewish Messiah is intrinsic to his role as the cosmic Lord of all.

Yeshua's most basic claim to being the cosmic Lord, the one to bear the name of the One God of Israel, is grounded in him first and foremost being the Messiah of Israel. As Sam Nadler writes:

> The New Covenant presents Yeshua as the Jewish Messiah (John 1:41 45, etc.). If He's not the Jewish Messiah, then no one should believe in Him, because His credentials to be the Savior of the World is based on His credentials as the Messiah of Israel. (Nadler first paragraph)

Yeshua is first and foremost the Jewish Messiah, the one to fulfill all of the Messianic prophecies and hopes of the Jewish People. The starting point of Yeshua's place as the Lord of All comes from his being the fulfillment of David's promise of an eternal heir to his throne—in fact, the greatest heir and the final Davidic king. As Messiah, the king and savior of the Jewish People, Yeshua has the sole right to be cosmic Lord over the whole of the created order, both seen and unseen (Schreiner *Hebrews* Heb. 1:3).

The right to rulership by Yeshua is grounded in his role fulfilling the promise made to Abraham, which said the Jewish People will be blessed as well as those people (nations) who bless the Jewish People (Gen. 12:3). The Abrahamic promise in turn would be fulfilled in the promise to David of an eternal, Messianic Davidic king, who will ultimately reign over Jew and Gentile.

In Romans 9:4-5 Paul asserted God's plan in cultivating and loving the Jewish People through whom he would bring the promise and reality of the Jewish Messiah:

> the people of Isra'el! They were made God's children, the Sh'khinah has been with them, the covenants are theirs, likewise the giving of the *Torah*, the Temple service and the promises; the Patriarchs are theirs; and from them, as far as his physical descent is concerned, came the Messiah, who is over all. Praised be *Adonai* for ever! Amen.

The starting point for Yeshua to be the Savior of the cosmos and cosmic Lord of the Nations begins first with his prophetical fulfillment of the promises made to the Jewish People. God's love for the world that he created was extended out from Israel to the Nations of the world. Paul further put forward that the ultimate fulfillment was Yeshua the Jewish Messiah, the bearer and initiator of the Good News which we see earlier in Paul's Letter to Rome where he spoke of the Jewish priority of the Good News and its extension to the Gentile world:

> … the Good News, … is God's powerful means of bringing salvation to everyone who keeps on trusting, to the Jew especially, but equally to the Gentile (Rom. 1:16).

John F. Walvoord helps to clarify the role of Yeshua in God's plan for redemption and divine universal rulership of the Messiah when he wrote:

> From the standpoint of God's divine election, Israel is… the key, and through Israel God was to fulfill His purpose whether redemptive, political, or eschatological (*Nations*, "History of Israel").

To the glory of God the Father

God the Father grants to Yeshua the Divine Name when he is declared to be *Adonai*, the Lord of all. Yeshua does not displace the Father but now shares with him in the Divine Name (MacLeod 44). The worship and praise to be offered to Yeshua as Lord is for the glory of God the Father. Rather than taking the place of God the Father in this closing line to the hymn, we see the acknowledgment that Yeshua receives the honor due only to the One God of Israel, as he is one with the Father. This place of Yeshua is from the Father and not something taken by Yeshua in a cosmic coup or replacement of the God of the *Tanakh* (Dunn 251).

This exaltation of Yeshua by the Father is related to the vision of Daniel 7 (Boyarin 32). In verse 9, we see that there are two thrones, one for the Ancient of Days (God the Father) and one for the Son of Man (Yeshua the Messiah). Later in verses 13 and 14, the Ancient of Days grants eternal, universal rulership to the Son of man in line with the exaltation of Yeshua by the Father we read about here in Philippians.

Paul's Call to Living the New Life in Messiah (2:12-18)

12 So, my dear friends, just as you have always obeyed when I was with you, it is even more important that you obey now when I am away from you: keep working out your deliverance with fear and trembling,

After Paul had set before the Philippians the ultimate model of humility, the Messiah Yeshua, who became a slave and willing sacrifice for the divine plan, he moves on to call the Philippians to practical modeling of the humble nature of the Messiah (Walvoord *Live* 49). As the founder of the Philippian faith community and Apostle to the Gentiles, Paul asserts his authority via a letter, which served as a proxy for his appearance in person, since he was imprisoned in Rome (Keener 561). Though he is separated by distance, he offers official words of instruction but he does so in love as evidenced by his referring to the Philippians as "my dear friends." His words display the intimacy and immediacy of the relationship Paul had created with the Philippian community when he had been there in person.

Paul's love for the Philippians flowed from his own love for God and obedience to God. As a Jew Paul had practiced Jewish

Torah observance through acts of obedience ordered by Torah. For the mostly Gentile, Philippian community, obedience would be different than for Messianic Jews in Philippi, but the same motivation of simple obedience would still apply. As we have seen above, Yeshua's own obedience to God and his plan, even death on the Roman stake, was to be the path for many of those who call Yeshua, Lord. (VanGemeren 43). This life of obedience to God is an ongoing obligation for Paul, who urges the Philippians to keep working on their salvation by continual spiritual growth, modeling the Messiah (Hawthorne 142).

---

13 for God is the one working among you both the willing and the working for what pleases him.

As the Philippians are being called to model Yeshua by Paul, he here demonstrates to the Philippians the importance of their work for Messiah by continuing the work of Messiah and also demonstrating the transformation in their lives as seen in John Walvoord's comments on Philippians 2:12:

> The work of Christ on the cross was only the beginning of the work of God for man. Rich as was its provision in the redemption provided for the entire world, the application of that redemption to the individual and the realization in spiritual experience of victory over sin involves a subsequent undertaking of God. God's method, using the work of Christ as the basis and the example of Christ as the pattern, is to reproduce in the life of the Christian the mind of Christ. The secret of this is bound up in the little phrase: "God worketh in you." … In verse twelve, however, it is presented as a Christian experience of manifesting the salvation which God provides in a life of victory and obedience (*Live* 49).

Paul here shares with the Philippians that all we seek to do in the service of God comes from God's grace (O'Callaghan 16). It is only by God's grace that followers of Yeshua can act righteously because it is in union with Yeshua that empowers right living. As this verse states it is God working in the Yeshua follower that gives empowerment for good works (Meyer 280–281).

The Complete Jewish Study Bible (1690) clarifies verse 13 from a Jewish perspective:

> This passage reveals a paradox of both human free will and God's foreknowledge. God is active, and not separate from his creation, yet his foreknowledge does not explicitly mean foreordination in that he grants humankind free will (Schechter, [*Aspects of Rabbinic* Judaism] 284–85). It would be a denial of God's own nature to not do the work that pleases him (Eph. 2:8–10). For, as stated by Rabbi Akiva, "All is foreseen, and free will is given" (Sacks, [*The Koren Pirke Avot*] 74–75; *Pirke Avot* 3:15).

---

14 Do everything without grumbling or arguing,

One of the major themes of the Philippian letter is a joyful unity within the community and clearly verse 14 addresses actions that could be antithetical. As he had called the Philippians earlier in the chapter to model the sacrificial giving of the Messiah, Paul continues here to stress that unity impacts the local community and also the outside world, which Paul terms "a twisted and perverted generation" in verse 15. It is in living without grumbling and disputing that unity can be reached in community. In laying aside these negative attitudes, the Philippians can stand renewed, unified in their community and be a positive example of Yeshua in the pagan world of Philippi (Bockmuehl 156). Yeshua is the supreme example of humility and for those in Philippi that Paul is calling to be more and more "in Messiah" the first important step is to remove all obstacles to pure living such as "grumbling and arguing," which represent the polar opposite of Yeshua's example.

15 so that you may be blameless and pure children of God, without defect in the midst of a twisted and perverted generation, among whom you shine like stars in the sky,

Paul is teaching the Philippians that as children of God, they are to live as lights—"to shine like stars"—in a dark world. The Jewish notion of light as a sign of righteousness derives from Daniel 12:3, for those who are righteous and call others to righteousness will shine like stars (Keener 561). Even earlier in Proverbs, we see the *Torah* being presented as light and by example, those who follow *Torah* will shine forth with the brightness of God's standard for right living:

> "For the *mitzvah* is a lamp, *Torah* is light, and reproofs
> that discipline is the way to life." (Prov. 6:23)

In later Jewish tradition we can see the connection between light and the righteous in Rashi's commentary on Genesis 1:4 where he wrote:

> AND GOD SAW THE LIGHT THAT IT WAS GOOD, AND GOD CAUSED A DIVISION—Here, also, we must depend upon the statement of the Agada: He saw that the wicked were unworthy of using it (the light); He, therefore, set it apart (ויבדל), reserving it for the righteous in the world to come. (Chagigah 12a) (Sefaria)

16 as you hold on to the Word of Life. If you do this, I will be able to boast, when the Day of the Messiah comes, that I did not run or toil for nothing.

The Word of Life is the Good News of Messiah Yeshua (O'Brien 296). In 1 Yochanan/ 1 John 1:1–3, we read an extended description of the "Word of Life":

The Word, which gives life!
He existed from the beginning.
We have heard him,
we have seen him with our eyes,
we have contemplated him,
we have touched him with our hands!

The life appeared,
and we have seen it.
We are testifying to it
and announcing it to you—
eternal life!

He was with the Father,
and he appeared to us.

What we have seen and heard,
we are proclaiming to you;
so that you too
may have fellowship with us.
Our fellowship is with the Father
and with his Son, Yeshua the Messiah.

Paul has invested his whole life since his encounter with Yeshua on the Road to Damascus to bringing the Good News of Yeshua to the Gentile world. The "boast" he envisions is in the assurance that after years of sacrifice and suffering, the Philippians will hold on to the Gospel until Yeshua returns.

Paul calls the Philippians to live lives shaped by walking within the Good News of Messiah so their lives of faithfulness will honor Paul's life of service to Yeshua. Part of his boasting lies in his resting in the reality of his faithful work coming to fruition in the changed lives through his ministry service (Merkle 159).

---

17 Indeed, even if my lifeblood is poured out as a drink offering over the sacrifice and service of your faith, I will still be glad and rejoice with you all.

Here Paul refers to his life being poured out as a "drink offering," a reference to the common practice of many ancient religions, including Judaism, to have drink offerings to God or the gods (Keener 561). Paul acknowledges his willingness to suffer and sacrifice on behalf of the Messiah, which he does with joy and also as an act of service to the Philippians. He is showing them a glowing example of what sincere love and service means in practical terms as he speaks to them in the letter. Paul is also looking at his impending execution and pictures his whole life of service to Yeshua as a figurative "drink offering"; his all has been poured out in his work of making Messiah known (Anders Phil. 2:17).

As Philippi was known for all of the temples and religious observances of false gods and the emperor cult, Paul's drink offering points to a new priesthood, a priesthood of the One God of Israel (Ware 274). Paul is being poured out as a sacrifice for them, and as Paul wrote in the letter to the Romans, followers of Yeshua must be willing to offer themselves as "living sacrifices" (Romans 12:1–2).

18 Likewise, you too should be glad and rejoice with me.

As the Philippians were to rejoice in God's work in the world being done through the suffering of Paul, they should find in their own sufferings opportunity to model their Messiah and to give glory to God for drawing them near his service and the future glory of the Messianic Age. This rejoicing is not about Paul's suffering and persecution for the sake of being persecuted in some self-destructive sense but in furthering the work of Yeshua in the world. As Paul rejoiced in his chains, it was not for the chains but the opportunity to make the Messiah known in new ways and to new people.

The Examples of Timothy and Epaphroditus (2:19-30)

As Paul called the Philippians to imitate the example of Yeshua, he now adds two other examples for them to model in their lives, Timothy and Epaphroditus (Aymer loc. 7643). The Philippians already knew both of these individuals.

The Example of Timothy (2:19–24)

19 But I hope in the Lord Yeshua to send Timothy to you shortly, so that I too may be cheered by knowing how you are doing.
20 I have no one who compares with him, who will care so sincerely for your welfare—

21 people all put their own interests ahead of the Messiah Yeshua's.

22 But you know his character, that like a child with his father he slaved with me to advance the Good News.

The Philippians already knew Timothy as a man of character and Paul knew that they could be confident in his impending service to them on behalf of Paul (Thielman 358). Timothy functioned as Paul's "son" in his ministry work. We do not know much about Timothy's biological father except that he was Greek (Acts 16:1) and apparently was not active in the life of Timothy, who seems to have been brought up by his mother and grandmother (2 Timothy 1:5) (Dobson 1511).

23 So I hope to send him just as soon as I see how things will go with me,

24 and I am confident in the Lord that before long I myself will come too.

In these verses, Paul expressed his hope to send Timothy to be with them. Paul even expressed the hope that he may be released from his imprisonment to make one final trip to Philippi to see the people that mean so much to him.

The Example of Epaphroditus (2:25–30)

25 Also I considered it necessary to send you Epaphroditus, my brother, fellow-worker and fellow-soldier, the emissary whom you sent to take care of my needs;

26 since he has been longing for you all and has been distressed because you heard he was ill.

27 Indeed he was ill, close to death; but God had mercy on him—and not only on him, but also on me—otherwise I would have had sorrow piled on sorrow.

28 Therefore, I am all the more eager to send him, so that you may rejoice when you see him again; and I, for my part, may be less sad.

29 So give him a joyful welcome in the Lord; honor such people.

30 For he risked his life and nearly died working for the Messiah, in order to give me the help you were not in a position to give.

The Philippians had sent Epaphroditus, a member of the Messianic community in Philippi, to serve Paul during his Roman imprisonment. We do not know why Paul sent Epaphroditus to Philippi though there has been a traditional understanding that he was sent back to Philippi with this letter (Lightner *Knowledge* Vol. 2 658). Another possibility for Paul to send Epahroditus back to Philippi was because the Philippians had heard of his illness and Paul wanted him to return to them in health to comfort their fears.

Robert Lightner expanded on Paul's feelings about Epaphroditus when he wrote:

But Paul wanted to be doubly sure the believers knew how highly he thought of Epaphroditus. He called him **my brother, fellow worker ... fellow soldier,** and **messenger**. He shared Paul's spiritual life, labors, and dangers. He willingly took the role of a servant to assist

Paul...This man, whose name means "charming,"served
the Lord while he served others.

While there with Paul in Rome, Epaphroditus became sick to
the point of death, possibly from the poor conditions of Paul's
life under house arrest in Rome. As he has recovered from his
illness and has served Paul well, this faithful worker is being
returned home to continue his service for Yeshua among the
Philippian Messianic Community.

Philippians 3

Not only that, but I consider everything a disadvantage in comparison with the supreme value of knowing the Messiah Yeshua as my Lord. It was because of him that I gave up everything and regard it all as garbage, in order to gain the Messiah and be found in union with him, not having any righteousness of my own based on legalism, but having that righteousness which comes through the Messiah's faithfulness, the righteousness from God based on trust.

—Philippians 3:8–9

Chapter Introduction

Chapter 3 begins with Paul's warning against false teachers. Depending on the scholar, these false teachers were either real individuals threatening the Gospel message in Philippi or they were potential false teachers who could be coming to Philippi now that the Gospel message was being spread among the Gentile populace.

A fresh, Messianic Jewish look at this chapter is important considering that the earliest Christian commentaries used this chapter as a polemic against Judaism and Jewish practice, specifically circumcision. Most notable are the fourth-century C.E. homilies of John Chrysostom, which have been the basis for the anti-Judaism bias prevalent in most current Philippians commentaries.

In this chapter Paul confronts false teaching from the opponents of the Good News of Messiah and rebukes false teaching from either heretical Yeshua followers or one of the many pagan proponents in Philippi who could lead the new Philippian believers away from their faith in Yeshua the Messiah.

Commentary

Conclusion? (3:1)

---

1 In conclusion, my brothers: rejoice in union with the Lord. It is no trouble for me to repeat what I have written you before, and for you it will be a safeguard:

This first verse in Chapter 3 is one of several "concluding" verses of the letter that have caused much debate. Some scholars hold that Philippians is an edited collection of two or more letters sent by Paul and this verse in the middle of the letter appears to offer evidence.

Rather than a "conclusion" to one of multiple letters, David H. Stern, however, suggests that Paul was summarizing a discussion of humility with a warning not to boast. As Yeshua in the Messianic hymn of Chapter 2 represented godly humility, Paul's opponents in Chapter 3 represent the opposite of humility—pride (Stern *Commentary* 598).

In commenting on this verse, Craig Keener (562) interprets the Greek word χαίρω (*chaire*), commonly translated as "in conclusion" or "finally," as a transition between sections within the letter. Jeffrey Reed (80–81) came to a similar conclusion that Philippians 3:1 is not the ending but a continuation of the letter. In fact, we will see in Chapter 3 a fourth example of selfless servanthood that promotes Messiah-like self-sacrifice and humility. Understood this way we can see the flow of the letter's theme of humility in the examples of Yeshua (2:5–11), Timothy (2:22), Epaphroditus (2:29), and now in Chapter 3, the example of Paul himself (Parsons 12).

Paul's Opponents (3:2–3)

2 beware of the dogs, those evildoers, the Mutilated!

We do not know the identity of the opponents Paul warned about here because he does not identify them by name but only refers to them by epithets. Most scholars understand the epithets to represent Jewish opponents and false teachers. For Paul to call these opponents "dogs" comes from the notion that it was believed that Jews used this term in referring to Gentiles; this understanding goes back to early Church father John Chrysostom's "Homilies on Philippians" (written in the fourth century c.e.).

The reference to "the mutilated," the Greek word being κατατομή (*katatome*), which most commentators see as a derogative reference to *b'rit milah* (ritual circumcision) in Judaism, can reinforce the belief that these opponents were Jews that Paul calls "mutilators" of the flesh.

Some scholars also see the word *katatome* as a reference to spiritual mutilation (Harlow 266), which may point to these false teachers being Gentiles, possible recent converts to Judaism, who were promoting circumcision of Gentiles. If so, such circumcision could represent both a physical mutilation and a spiritual mutilation. This seemingly negative understanding of circumcision and Jewish practice has led many commentators to understand Paul here in Philippians 3 and elsewhere as being against Judaism and *Torah*. For example, in the HarperCollins Study Bible at Philippians 3:2, a footnote states that the reference to *katatome* is a harsh rejection of circumcision for all followers of Yeshua. This reading rejects the ongoing practice of circumcision for Jewish followers and makes Paul's use of *katatome* into a polemic against Judaism and Torah observance (Attridge and Meeks Phil. 3:2).

Most commentators see this verse and the following verses in Chapter 3 as demonstrating Paul's rejection of Judaism and Jewish practice. In refreshing contrast stands Mark Nanos, who is one of the only scholars to question the credibility that Paul, a Jew, would use derogatory language about Judaism and *Torah*-faithful Jews, whether within or without the Messianic community (*Corinthians* 111).

There are those like Bockmuehl (6) and Boring (228) who see the opponents of Paul as not actual but potential opponents, with Paul pre-emptively warning the Philippians about false teachers that could come to Philippi. These "opponents" are then potential threats to the growing Philippian community about whom Paul preemptively warned the Philippians.

Whoever the opponents were they represented an opposite mindset and lifestyle to that of Yeshua, Paul, Timothy, and Epaphroditus as Herbert W. Bateman IV (59), commented:

The depiction of these opponents as self-centered ("god is their belly," ὁ θεὸς ἡ κοιλία), self-gratifying ("their glory is in their shame," ἡ δόξα ἐν τῇ αἰσχύνῃ), and worldly ("who set their minds on earthly things," τὰ ἐπίγεια φρονοῦντες) clearly contrasts the self-denying, self-giving, self-sacrificing attitude and life of Jesus (2:6–8) and the lifestyles of Timothy (2:20–23), Epaphroditus (2:25–29), and Paul (3:7–16).

The proposed identities for Paul's opponents include Yeshua-following Jews (Messianic Jews), non-Yeshua-following Jews, newly converted proselytes, and pagan influencers. Let's examine the evidence for these four possible identities.

Yeshua-following Jews/Messianic Jews

The first option is that these opponents are Messianic Jews who did not accept the ruling of the Jerusalem Council (see Acts 15) and who were promoting circumcision on Philippian Gentiles that became followers of Yeshua. These opponents could be the same people that Paul spoke against in the letter to the Galatians (Hansen 217).

Most Christian scholars understand the opponents were promoting conversion for Gentiles, which would have forced Judaism and Jewish customs on Gentiles for the first time since the birth of the Messianic movement. Messianic Jewish scholars and post-supersessionist scholars would see this as detrimental to the unique place of Jews and Gentiles within the Messianic community (and certainly counter to the Acts 15 Jerusalem Council ruling, which recommended separate ritual responsibilities for Jews and Gentiles).

These opponents are classically known as "Judaizers" (Jewish proponents of Gentile circumcision). Given that from the time of Abraham the sign of the covenant between the One God of Israel and the Jewish People has been circumcision, these opponents incorrectly championed the circumcision of Gentiles as we see in Schreiner:

> Therefore, the Judaizers probably concluded from Genesis 17 (see also Exod. 4:24–26; Lev. 12:3; Josh. 5:2–9) that circumcision was an indispensable sign of the covenant, and thus they taught that "unless you are circumcised according to the custom of Moses, you cannot be saved." (Acts 15:1) (*Dictionary* "Circumcision")

Paula Fredriksen espoused a unique motivation for these Messianic Jews to promote circumcision of Gentile Yeshua-followers:

> Or perhaps some of these apostles, prioritizing Israel's response to the gospel as the key event leading to the Kingdom, sought "Israel" among the nations quite literally…Perhaps, then, in calling for (gentile) circumcision as a condition for entry into the ekklesia, these apostles were in their own minds achieving the reconstitution of the plenum of Israel. With all Israel regathered through the message of the messiah, the Kingdom could, finally, come (cf. Rom 11.26) (*Pagans* 104–105).

According to Fredriksen, these promoters of Gentile circumcision were seeking to make the Messianic communities "more Jewish" by having the Gentile male followers be circumcised and all Gentile followers become Jews.

Understood this way, the proponents of Gentile circumcision were seeking to reclaim the Jewish nature of the Yeshua movement by attempting to make all adherents Jews by adding new Gentile converts to Judaism to the born Jews, making the Messianic Community again a Jewish majority. This concern for reaching "all Israel", including turning Gentile Yeshua-followers into Jews via conversion allowed the false teachers to seek circumcision of Gentile Yeshua followers to make the movement more Jewish.

Paul was not giving a polemic against Judaism or Jewish practice but was condemning a false teaching that Gentiles needed to become Jews to follow Yeshua. Paul rejected false teaching within the Yeshua movement (Fredriksen, *Pagans* 100) and not Judaism, especially circumcision for Jews. Paul himself was circumcised and he had also circumcised the adult Timothy before the beginning of their mission to bring the Gospel to Macedonia. The problem of Gentile circumcision for Paul was his opposition to the false teaching that Yeshua-believing Gentiles must undergo circumcision for inclusion into the community and also that Yeshua faith was not sufficient for Gentiles and needed supplementation with circumcision—a false teaching the Jerusalem Council had already ruled against in Acts 15.

Non-Yeshua-following Jews

Since we see in Paul's first visit to Philippi (Acts 16) that the Jewish Community was not large enough to have a synagogue, Paul's opponents would not likely have included members of the local Jewish Community.

Newly Converted Proselytes

David H. Stern understood Paul's opponents as Gentile converts to Judaism who were expressing pride as circumcised Gentile Yeshua followers in Philippi compared to the uncircumcised Gentile followers (Stern *Commentary* 598–599). These proponents of circumcision were seeking to convince those in Philippi that they would have a higher status as Yeshua believers by their circumcision. Beyond violating the Jerusalem Council's ruling that Gentiles did not need to become Jews but could be full members of the Messianic Community and grafted into the People of God as Gentiles, these opponents were also expressing pride, the opposite of the humility that Paul exhorts to the Philippians as followers of Yeshua.

Pagan Influencers

Mark Nanos challenges the identification of Paul's opponents being Jews (Yeshua-following or Non-Yeshua-following) or recent converts to Judaism and instead, puts forward that these opponents are from local religious cults and philosophical groups, such as the Cynics who were local to Philippi. These local cults and pagan influencers posed a challenge to the Gentile Yeshua followers in Philippi who were navigating their new life as followers of the One God of Israel and living in a Jewish sub-group (the Yeshua movement) while remaining non-Jews (*Polemic* 5). As a faithful Jew, Paul would not oppose Judaism but he would speak against pagan or cultic false religion (Horsley 6–7).

Herbert Ulonska, cited by Mark Nanos, understood these opponents of Paul as pagans castrated in one of the various orgiastic cults in Philippi who thought their castration was like circumcision that would allow them into the Messianic Community (*Corinthians* 112).

Nanos noted that one of these possible pagan influences that Paul may have warned about was the Cybele cult, which, in practice, met all three of Paul's warnings:

> A newly developed festival introduced Attis—Cybele's consort, who bled to death after castrating himself for Cybele—into the Roman cult. On the "day of blood" the galli [eunuch priests of the Phrygian goddess Cybele] flagellated themselves while engaged in frenzied, ecstatic dancing, while the initiates castrated themselves with a shard. Castration of galli would represent a clear case of "mutilation" and of figures whom Paul would likely regard as "evil workers," perhaps even as behaving like dogs in a general derogatory sense, if not also specifically involving dogs or dog imagery (*Corinthians* 161–162).

Other pagan influencers in Philippi included groups that used dogs as religious icons in the worship of Silvanus, Diana, and Hecate and groups that used dogs in sacrifices and magical rituals; one group, the Cynics, was even known as "the dogs" (Nanos *Corinthians* 118–119).

For new Yeshua-followers in Philippi to continue to be accepted in Philippian society, they may have been tempted to adopt a common syncretic way of worship and add either former pagan ways or add new pagan ways to their new Yeshua faith. Being influenced to convert to Judaism by either Yeshua-following Jews, non-Yeshua following Jews, or Gentile converts to Judaism would not seem to bring new followers any advantage in Philippi, especially considering Paul and Silas' imprisonment recorded in Acts 16. If the false teachers had some higher status in Philippian society, it does not appear that Jewish identity would be as helpful compared to one of the pagan options.

Paul's Positions

While Paul rejected the circumcision of male, Gentile Yeshua followers, he clearly endorsed the unique place Jews and Gentiles played in the Body of Messiah, which included his continuing support for Jewish male circumcision as demonstrated by his circumcising Timothy. Paul based the Good News he preached on the unity within the diversity of the Body of Messiah. Gentiles as Gentiles joining with the Jewish People to worship the One God of Israel represented the fulfillment of the Messianic hope in the person of Yeshua (Nanos *Within* 19). Such a joining together as fellow worshippers shows the opening of relationship to the One God of Israel for all humanity (Nanos *Within* 110).

Rather than against Judaism and Jewish practices such as circumcision, Paul speaks against other Yeshua followers seeking to impose circumcision on Gentile converts to the Messianic faith. We then have an intra-Messianic debate and not a polemic against Judaism and Jewish practice by Jews—such a polemic, unfortunately, has been the common interpretation since the second century c.e. to today (Fredriksen *Pagans* 99–100). Most Christian commentators view this verse as Paul's blanket opposition to circumcision for Yeshua-following Jews, especially since the Greek word *katatome* used in this verse is translated as "mutilated" or "mutilators."

Paul is not speaking against *b'rit-milah* (circumcision) of Jewish males at eight days old, (note that Paul speaks positively of his own *b'rit-milah* in verse 5 below), but specifically against those false teachers who want to impose ritual circumcision on Gentile men after coming to believe in Yeshua as Messiah and Lord (Nanos *Within* 10).

---

3 For it is we who are the Circumcised, we who worship by the Spirit of God and make our boast in the Messiah Yeshua! We do not put confidence in human qualifications,

---

We who are the Circumcised

Other translations exist for this verse, for example, the English Standard Version (ESV) uses "For we are the real circumcision," a reference to all Yeshua followers now having "spiritual circumcision," which is a replacement for the physical act of *b'rit milah* (ritual circumcision). Though there is biblical precedence for "spiritual circumcision," the error here by most Christian commentators is in teaching that "spiritual circumcision" replaces or supersedes physical circumcision, which is still a continuing covenantal act for Jews.

Most commentaries apply this replacement of physical circumcision to spiritual circumcision to both Jews and Gentiles as a polemic against physical circumcision—even going as far as seeing baptism as a New Covenant replacement for circumcision, which makes infant baptism so prominent in Catholic and some Protestant churches.

Barry Horner pointed out that the translation of this verse as "the real circumcision" in the English Standard Version (ESV)

or "the true circumcision" in the Revised Standard Version (RSV) reflects replacement theology/supersessionism (Horner 26). The ESV interpretation and rendering of Philippians 3:3 essentially states that Paul teaches physical circumcision/*b'rit-milah* is now a former act of a now former nation of Israel. Horner (275) further commented:

> This I believe to be a mistaken understanding of Paul's overall teaching. According to Paul's own confession, he remained a distinctive, bona fide Jew after he became a Christian (Acts 16:1-3; 22:3; Rom 9:3-4; 11:1).

We who worship by the Spirit of God and make our boast in the Messiah Yeshua!

We see Paul here speaking of a new Spirit-infused worship to which he calls the Philippians to participate—in contrast to many of his contemporary Jews who believed the Spirit of God had ceased to work in the world. Paul clarified that Yeshua, as the Messiah of Israel, had inaugurated the world to come and the return of Spirit activity in the current day (Keener 563).

We do not put confidence in human qualifications,

Paul warned against "confidence in human qualifications" (including physical circumcision), preferring to "boast in Messiah Yeshua." The life of the follower should be focused on Yeshua and divine worship and service. We will see more from Paul on human qualifications in the next three verses.

Paul's Response to the Opponents (3:4–11)

Paul's Jewish Résumé (3:4–6)

---

4 even though I certainly have grounds for putting confidence in such things. If anyone else thinks he has grounds for putting confidence in human qualifications, I have better grounds:

5 • b'rit-milah on the eighth day,
  • by birth belonging to the people of Isra'el,
  • from the tribe of Binyamin,
  • a Hebrew-speaker, with Hebrew-speaking parents,
  • in regard to the Torah, a Parush,

6 • in regard to zeal, a persecutor of the Messianic Community,
  • in regard to the righteousness demanded by legalism, blameless.

Many commentators see these verses as a way for Paul to out-credential the opponents who are advocating for Gentile circumcision (and *Torah* observance for Gentiles) by putting forward his spectacular "Jewish résumé." Rather than seeking to out-credential his opponents, Paul here is placing before them his authority as the teacher of these Philippian Gentiles. Paul is instructing them about their new life within Jewish life as Gentiles and his authority over those opponents who are trying to bring the Philippian Yeshua-followers into conformity with their former pagan life and the norms of society (Nanos *Polemic* 8).

Paul clarifies that not only is he a Jew, but he is a Jew

par excellence. We see that he comes from observant parents who had him circumcised on the eighth day to observe *Torah* commands. According to Theodoret, cited in the *Ancient Christian Commentary on Scripture*, Paul bolstered his authority by specifying his descent from Benjamin, the son of Rachel, Jacob's beloved wife (Edwards Phil. 3:5a).

In these verses, Paul speaks of his connection to and zealous practice of Judaism. He was a student of the great Jewish sage Gamaliel (Acts 22:3) and sought to advance in his learning and practice of Judaism to exceed his peers (Gal. 1:14) to prove himself as a faithful and zealous Jew for *Torah* (Bahnsen 95). Paul here showed no dissatisfaction concerning his life as a Jew, as one who practiced Judaism with zeal, even going as far as claiming to be "blameless" about *Torah* (Nanos *View* 176).

According to David Friedman (4), Paul speaks in the *present tense* of his life as a *Parush* (Pharisee) when presenting his "Jewish résumé." Paul's zealousness motivated him to succeed in his traditional Jewish studies as he sought the highest level of *Torah* observance taught by his teachers (Verhoef 42). Paul underscored in Galatians 1:14 that his zealousness included his zeal for the Oral *Torah*, the traditions passed down by his ancestors (Ehrensperger 14). Unfortunately, he also admits that his zealousness for his religious practice led him to persecute the followers of Yeshua and seek to destroy the early Messianic Jewish Community.

In the detailed listing of his Jewish credentials, Paul expresses "confidence" in them in verse 4. We also see Paul's abiding connection as a Jew to his Jewish People when he warmly describes them in Romans 9:4–5, as we read before in

Chapter 2, but these verses are worth repeating here:

> the people of Isra'el! They were made God's children, the Sh'khinah has been with them, the covenants are theirs, likewise the giving of the *Torah*, the Temple service and the promises; the Patriarchs are theirs; and from them, as far as his physical descent is concerned, came the Messiah, who is over all. Praised be *Adonai* for ever! Amen.

In stating that he is "a Hebrew-speaker, with Hebrew-speaking parents," Paul emphasized that he lived within a Hebrew-speaking family and community and therefore, had a higher status than Diaspora Jews (Stern *Commentary* 600). Paul stresses to his opponents, who focused on human qualifications, that he had better qualifications than they did, which could indicate his opponents were converts to Judaism. Paul points out his lifelong Jewish status as well as his status as a Hebrew-speaking Jew.

Paul's listing of his Jewish credentials and heritage in Philippians 3:4–6 and in Romans 9:4–5 brings to mind the Passover song "Dayenu." In this song sung during the Passover *seder*, we see a progression of 15 miracles performed by God for the Jewish People:

> 1) If He had brought us out of Egypt. 2) If He had executed justice upon the Egyptians. 3) If He had executed justice upon their gods. 4) If He had slain their first-born. 5) If He had given to us their health and wealth. 6) If He had split the sea for us. 7) If He had led us through on dry land. 8) If He had drowned our oppressors. 9) If He had provided for our needs in the wilderness for 40 years. 10) If He had fed us manna. 11) If He had given us Shabbat. 12) If

He had led us to Mount Sinai. 13) If He had given us the Torah. 14) If He had brought us into the Land of Israel. 15) If He built the Temple for us. (Dayenu!)

Following the recitation of each of these miraculous events is a chorus of "Dayenu," a Hebrew word meaning "that would have been enough" (Eisenberg 3). The recitation of each of the miracles, from being brought out of Egypt to the building of the Holy Temple in Jerusalem, would, in its own right, be a sufficient blessing "that would have been enough" from the God of Israel to the People of Israel.

Paul is likewise listing his Jewish credentials (minus his persecution of believers) as blessings from God, each of which is of great value, such as each of the miracles in the song, which can stand alone as miraculous acts of love for Israel by God with each new miracle being even more of a blessing. As we will see in verse 8, Paul's greatest "Dayenu" blessing in his life is knowing Messiah and following Yeshua; everything else about his life and heritage is valuable and a divine blessing but they do not compare with the revelation of Yeshua in his life. After an extensive listing of all that he can boast about in his "Jewish résumé" and all that he had from birth and practice, Paul made clear to the Philippians that his only source of true "confidence" was in Yeshua, living in union with Messiah as his sole focus (Thompson 7).

The Cost of Knowing Messiah (3:7–11)

7 But the things that used to be advantages for me, I have, because of the Messiah, come to consider a disadvantage.

Paul realized that in Yeshua everything else pales and that in this new life his relationship with God was no longer based on his actions, "human qualifications," and even his genuine Jewish background, but instead, life is in Yeshua as Robert Sloan stated:

> And Paul says that he realized—having realized that the Messiah had come and that the Messiah by God's plan and purpose had suffered sacrificially for us and been raised from the dead to start a new creation—Paul realized that those things that he was depending upon in the past were not sufficient to save (Sloan Unit 1S Sec. 6).

For Paul, knowing the Messiah and being integrated into the life of Yeshua has so transformed him that his whole identity from the time of his encounter with Yeshua on the Damascus Road is now wholly about becoming more and more "in Messiah." The core of his life is the transformation he had in his experience of coming to know Yeshua as the Messiah of Israel (Cousar *Reading* 170).

Everything else in his life, including his sterling "Jewish résumé," cannot compare with his incorporation into the Messiah (Hawthorne 182). His life itself is no longer his, but he now lives solely connected to and empowered by the Messiah. We can see this more fully in Galatians 2:20:

> When the Messiah was executed on the stake as a criminal, I was too; so that my proud ego no longer lives. But the Messiah lives in me, and the life I now live in my body I live by the same trusting faithfulness that the Son of God had, who loved me and gave himself up for me.

Rather than looking at his pre-Yeshua life in Judaism negatively, Paul is now in Messiah looking back on his whole life and reevaluating all of his life compared to knowing Messiah. He does not look back on his life before knowing the Messiah negatively, a conversion from Judaism to Christianity, but a new experience of Judaism and *Torah* life in Messiah (Campbell 90). His life in Judaism is entirely in Yeshua without rejecting his past.

We can see Paul here in his use of "advantage"/"disadvantage" using similar language to Yeshua's in Matthew 16:26:

> "What good will it do someone if he gains the whole world but forfeits his life? Or, what can a person give in exchange for his life?"

Here Yeshua is contrasting gaining the entire world (a great advantage, but at the great cost or loss of one's life). Unlike the person in Yeshua's example that chose advantages in this world over life in the world to come, Paul considers all of no advantage for the supreme knowledge of union with Yeshua (Hawthorne 188).

---

8 Not only that, but I consider everything a disadvantage in comparison with the supreme value of knowing the Messiah Yeshua as my Lord. It was because of him I gave up everything and regard it all as garbage, to gain the Messiah.

As Paul had previously looked upon Yeshua and the Messianic Community as worthless garbage, after his experience on the Damascus Road, he can now see Yeshua and the Messianic Community as supremely valuable.

Paul here makes a comparison in how he regards his Jewish identity as garbage compared to knowing Messiah. Both were highly valuable, but the new revelation made the new thing even more valuable (Rowland 191). Paul experienced knowing Yeshua as Messiah and Lord, the spiritual union of Paul with the Messiah and incorporation into Him (Loh 100).

Though many commentators interpret this verse as Paul's complete rejection of Judaism, a better understanding is that to Paul everything else in his life, even his heritage as a *Torah*-faithful Jew, paled by comparison to knowing Messiah, even being considered "rubbish." Stanley Stowers put it this way:

> Paul's narrative no more regards his past Jewish life as worthless than the exalted prerogatives that Christ gave up should be regarded as worthless. Rather, the first pales in comparison with the second. (120)

For N.T. Wright, Paul left behind his life as a Pharisee so that now his life was "in Messiah" and no longer in the Pharisaic world (*Resurrection* 233–234), though Paul's own words of defense before King Agrippa near the end of his life showed Paul touting his Jewish bona fides:

> "So then! All Jews know how I lived my life from my youth on, both in my own country and in Yerushalayim. They have known me for a long time; and if they are willing, they can testify that I have followed the strictest party in our religion—that is, I have lived as a *Parush*." (Acts 26:4–5)

Perhaps 1 Corinthians 9:20-21 best clarifies Paul's relationship with *Torah*. While affirming in verse 20 he is "not in subjection to a legalistic perversion of the *Torah*," Paul does declare he is "not outside the framework of God's *Torah* but within the framework of *Torah* as upheld by the Messiah." Paul is a Jew who has found the fulfillment of the Jewish Messianic hope in Yeshua. In embracing Yeshua, Paul did not become a non-Jew but a different Jew, a Jew that followed Yeshua (Rowland 19). His embracing of Yeshua as his Messiah and Lord makes everything else in his life of lesser value. Paul now sees even those things of highest value including his spectacular Jewish heritage and practice of Judaism as valueless compared to knowing Yeshua and experiencing the new life that comes from union with the Messiah; "gaining Messiah" is to Paul so profound and transformative that all else drops in comparative value (Bockmuehl 20).

From this time forward Paul continues living as a *Torah*-faithful Jew (as described above in 1 Corinthians 9:21) only now he does so as a Jew seeking to be more and more like the Messiah. Paul could say with conviction:

> "Brothers, although I have done nothing against either our people or the traditions of our fathers, I was made a prisoner in Yerushalayim and handed over to the Romans." (Acts 28:17)

Paul made this statement near the time he wrote Philippians (based on the understanding the letter was written during Paul's final imprisonment in Rome). Before the accusing Jewish leaders, Paul declared his faithfulness to the *Torah* and even "the traditions of our fathers." These traditions, also known as "the Oral *Torah*," would later be codified in the Mishnah (Friedman 49).

Paul understood that in Messiah his righteousness no longer depended on his work and observance but the righteousness he attained by placing his faith in Yeshua (Hansen 23). Paul could continue living as a Jew knowing Messiah was the source of his righteousness and that he could live out his life as an act of obedience alone and not to attain righteousness.

Paul now fully depended on the righteousness of his Lord. From his encounter with Yeshua on the Road to Damascus, Paul was on a lifelong journey to know Messiah more. Paul knew at the completion of his journey lay the Messiah and life eternal, and all that he lost for that gain was well worth whatever was ahead (Hawthorne 193).

What Paul gave up to know Messiah could be his former career path in the larger Jewish world as a Pharisee trained at the feet of Gamaliel, the great sage. Paul had before him the possibility of great honor and respect as one of the great Jewish teachers and leaders, even following his teacher Gamaliel as a leader in the Sanhedrin, but he let this path go to choose another one that led toward Yeshua. His choice was between being a respected sage and leader in the larger Jewish world or a persecuted emissary of Messiah Yeshua, and he chose the latter (Friedman 11).

Paul uses his rhetorical gifting to make clear to the Philippians the extreme value of knowing Yeshua and being incorporated into the Messianic Community, which can render all worthless in comparison, even referring to his pre-Yeshua life as "garbage" (Hawthorne 183).

Early Church father John Chrysostom's "Homilies on Philippians" (written in the fourth century c.e.) have been the basis for much of the anti-Judaism interpretations of

Philippians, yet in his homily on this verse, he provides an interesting analogy that can help us understand Paul's need to differentiate and choose:

> For as a poor man, that was in hunger, as long as he has silver, escapes hunger, but when he finds gold, and it is not allowable to keep both, considers it loss to retain the former, and having thrown it away, takes the gold coin; so also here; not because the silver is loss, for it is not; but because it is impossible to take both at once, but it is necessary to leave one (235).

---

9 and be found in union with him, not having any righteousness of my own based on legalism, but having that righteousness which comes through the Messiah's faithfulness, the righteousness from God based on trust.

Paul here states that the one thing of supreme value, rendering everything else worthless, is knowing Yeshua and gaining righteousness before God based on his trust and not on his human endeavors (Bates 16). It is by his union with the Messiah that he knows he now has righteousness based on the Messiah's faithfulness.

Paul expresses his hope in his union with Messiah given that Paul has been granted the righteousness of Messiah by his trust in Yeshua (Verhoef 42). Paul knows now it is the righteousness of Messiah (not his own) that made him right with God (Sanders *Law* 44–45).

Paul had found the Messiah, the One to bring redemption to Israel and the nations. Paul's life radically changed from being a persecutor of Yeshua and his *talmidim* (disciples) to being a proclaimer of the message of Yeshua to the Gentile world. This union with Yeshua compelled Paul to devote the rest of his life to serving the Messiah.

To those in Philippi who taught that righteousness before God was through *Torah* observance (and those today who teach the same), Paul here is clarifying that right standing with God is solely in union with the Messiah. Righteousness before God is only available through the atoning work of Yeshua, where he exchanged our sinfulness for his righteousness (Thielman 360).

In Yeshua, God stepped into history and provided a way for final right standing for those who trust in Yeshua as Messiah and Lord, which we see in Jeremiah's prophetic words (Thielman 360) where he wrote:

> "The days are coming," says *Adonai*, "when I will raise a righteous Branch for David. He will reign as king and succeed; he will do what is just and right in the land. In his days Y'hudah will be saved, Isra'el will live in safety, and the name given to him will be *Adonai Tzidkenu* [*Adonai* our righteousness]. (Jer. 23:5–6)

Paul here is making sure, via his own experience, that the Philippians know the righteousness of God is available only in Yeshua. Any effort at seeking righteousness before God outside of Yeshua falls short. In Romans, Paul spoke of the righteousness of the observant Jewish community:

> Brothers, my heart's deepest desire and my prayer to God for Isra'el is for their salvation; for I can testify to their zeal for God. But it is not based on correct understanding;

for, since they are unaware of God's way of making people righteous and instead seek to set up their own, they have not submitted themselves to God's way of making people righteous. For the goal at which the Torah aims is the Messiah, who offers righteousness to everyone who trusts. (Rom. 10:1-4)

Paul's point in Philippians 3:9 is that the only righteousness that he (and the Philippians) need is in their trust in Yeshua and not righteousness through their endeavors, even in circumcision or other actions on their part.

---

10 Yes, I gave it all up in order to know him, that is, to know the power of his resurrection and the fellowship of his sufferings as I am being conformed to his death,

---

Paul reflects on what he gave up as stated above, considering all that he had previously valued in his life, even his spectacular "Jewish résumé" to fully know Yeshua and to model himself like his Messiah (Hansen 231). We can see Paul here acknowledging that in Yeshua he has received what Moses (Exod. 33:13) and other prophets had hoped: the reality of intimately knowing God because of the work of Yeshua on his behalf (Keener 564). This reality even included taking on suffering like his Master.

It is in seeking to more fully know Yeshua and experience the power of the resurrection life in Messiah that has become Paul's soul passion. Considering his Damascus Road experience, Paul's life was a continuous striving to conform himself to the Messiah to gain the resurrection that only Yeshua offered (Anders 244).

11 so that somehow I might arrive at being resurrected from the dead.

Paul here is not questioning his eternal destiny. Paul here is stressing the importance of his own actively striving to model Yeshua in life, and he commends this same striving to the Philippians (Stern *Commentary* 601). Paul understood that the goal of his life was the resurrection and eternal life with Yeshua:

> I don't think the sufferings we are going through now are even worth comparing with the glory that will be revealed to us in the future. (Rom. 8:18)

The New Life in Messiah (3:12–17)

12 It is not that I have already obtained it or already reached the goal—no, I keep pursuing it in the hope of taking hold of that for which the Messiah Yeshua took hold of me. **13** Brothers, I, for my part, do not think of myself as having yet gotten hold of it; but one thing I do: forgetting what is behind me and straining forward toward what lies ahead, **14** I keep pursuing the goal in order to win the prize offered by God's upward calling in the Messiah Yeshua.

Paul's life was an active desire to more and more model his Messiah as he keeps striving more and more to grow in his faith and practice. Though he knows his eternal destiny is sure in Messiah, he knows he has yet to complete his journey of faith and service and therefore, keeps striving for the completion of his spiritual journey (Verhoef 43–44).

According to Craig Keener (564), Paul uses at least two common cultural references from the world of the Philippians. First, Paul uses the language of athletic competition when speaking of his attempt to become more like the Messiah and reach his goal of being with the Messiah for eternity. Second, Paul adapts the language of Greco-Roman philosophers who would discuss not being perfect but always in progression toward the goal of perfection.

To Paul, life is an ongoing journey of becoming more and more in Messiah and modeling the life and suffering of his Master. In this he was always looking forward to more knowledge of Yeshua and more opportunity for service to him. Knowing Yeshua more was a lifelong goal and pursuit and though he can rejoice at his past and how God has worked in his life and his achievements for building the Messianic Community, his sole focus was moving forward to be more and more like the Messiah. We can see his intense desire to become more and more in Messiah in his use of "straining" to describe his pursuit of Yeshua-likeness (Ash Phil. 3:13).

Athletic competitions, especially races, would also involve straining forward toward the finish line. In addition, the winner would receive a visible prize to stand out before the people. The prize Paul seeks is to fully know the Messiah and the life he can only achieve in Messiah. (Keener 564).

---

15 Therefore, as many of us as are mature, let us keep paying attention to this; and if you are differently minded about anything, God will also reveal this to you. **16** Only let our conduct fit the level we have already reached. **17** Brothers, join in imitating me, and pay attention to those who live according to the pattern we have set for you.

In these verses Paul now switches from first person to more inclusive language and pronouns—first- and second-person plural. He calls on others who are "mature" to maintain their level of conduct. He invites the Philippians to "join in imitating me."

The Way of Destruction (3:18–19)

18 For many—I have told you about them often before, and even now I say it with tears—live as enemies of the Messiah's execution-stake.

Paul here speaks about those who neglect or even downplay the importance of the Messiah's death on the scandalous Roman stake. The most disgraceful way to die at this time was by crucifixion, the punishment for slaves and criminals. For Gentiles it was a scandal to die such a death and for Jews it was the death for those cursed by God:

> If someone has committed a capital crime and is put to death, then hung on a tree, his body is not to remain all night on the tree, but you must bury him the same day, because a person who has been hanged has been cursed by God—so that you will not defile your land, which ADONAI your God is giving you to inherit. (Deut. 21:22–23)

Paul warns against those people who rejected the shameful death that the Messiah died for them to gain salvation. Out of their aversion to Yeshua's suffering and despised death, some people would not speak about it. The embracing of the scandal of a crucified Savior—so counter to Greco-Roman thought—

was an issue for the primarily Gentile Messianic Community; the Philippians would face opposition from those without and even within to their new faith in Yeshua (Keown Vol. 1 55). Paul warns that those who did not accept the despised death of Yeshua were rejecting the atonement offered to them and even more were enemies of the very sacrificial death that brought them new life.

Such aversion to the shameful death of the Messiah could even lead them to deny the faith they once had accepted. Those who turned away from their trust in Yeshua as the Messiah and were truly "living as enemies of the Messiah's execution-stake" had once been part of the Messianic Community but now they lived for themselves and not for Messiah (Bockmuehl 232).

Other enemies may have been less overt in their aversion; they may have simply not been walking in the example of the Messiah. Although Paul throughout Philippians, especially in the Messianic hymn of Chapter 2, emphasized the importance of modeling humility and self-sacrifice, some Yeshua "followers" could have been living self-centered lives while still claiming to follow Yeshua. Rather than outright rejection of their faith by their lifestyle, they opposed the model of the Messiah, making them enemies of the Messiah's execution stake as they refused to follow the example set for them (Hansen 264).

---

19 They are headed for destruction! Their god is the belly; they are proud of what they ought to be ashamed of, since they are concerned about the things of the world.

Many commentators understand this verse to be related to those mentioned earlier in the chapter in verse 2, commonly called "Judaizers," who promoted not only circumcision of Gentile Yeshua-followers but also Jewish dietary laws; hence, "their God is the belly," may have referred to incorrectly "worshipping" the kosher dietary laws (Melick 4).

However, Mark Keown (Vol.1 55) disagrees that Paul would refer to Jews as having their stomach as their god, which would contravene Paul's observance of Judaism and his respect for his fellow Jews seeking to follow the One God of Israel. G.W. Hansen (266) concurred with Keown that Paul was not speaking about Jews or Jewish practice:

> Paul uses the term stomach to represent "unbridled sensuality, whether gluttony or sexual licentiousness." For those who have no higher authority for the way they live than the dictates of their bodily appetites, their god is their stomach. They worship their appetites.
>
> Even though serving bodily appetites leads to shameful behavior, these people take pride in their shame; they broadcast and brag about their shameful indulgence of their physical appetites: their glory is in their shame.

Rather than discussing false teachers speaking about Jewish practice, Paul may have instead warned against local Philippians observing pagan practices, not surprising since Philippi was a heavily pagan-influenced city. (Also, most likely Paul is continuing his discussion of the "enemies" he rebukes in the immediately preceding verse 18.)

Let's look at some of the Philippian and Roman pagan practices at the time. Interestingly, when Paul first visited

Philippi, as recorded in Acts 16, he encountered a slave girl possessed by a "python spirit" whom her owners used as a fortune teller to make money. This same type of possession was common among the priests of Cybele as Mark Nanos noted:

> Divine possession for the Cybele priests was made speaking with strange voices emanating from their bellies ("belly-talker" or "belly-prophet" [engastrimantis], or "ventriloquists" who speak or prophesy from a demon inside of themselves [engastrimythos]). This is considered synonymous with "Pythones." (Nanos *Corinthians* 162–163)

In view of the above, "their god is their belly" is a perfect phrase for Paul to use to rebuke Philippian pagan people and practices. Understood this way, such an interpretation contrasts sharply with other commentaries that see verse 19 as an anti-Judaism polemical passage. Paul exhorts his former pagans who have embraced the Jewish Messiah not to compromise and return to the old ways of Philippian pagan religion. Paul cautions them not to adopt pagan practices that may provide temporary benefits and acceptance in contrast to accepting their new lives within a new Jewish context as one standing outside the pagan world and waiting for the life to come in their new heavenly citizenship.

The Way of Life (3:20-21)

20 But we are citizens of heaven, and it is from there that we expect a Deliverer, the Lord Yeshua the Messiah.

After telling the Philippians above about the punishment ("destruction" per Paul) for those who were enemies of Messiah, Paul promises them that as followers of Messiah they are now truly citizens of Heaven (Taylor 66) and are waiting for the return of the Messiah to bring this new citizenship to complete reality. As the Philippians highly valued their Roman citizenship, Paul here reminds them they hold even greater citizenship as followers of Yeshua—that is, heavenly citizenship (Boring 228).

In declaring Yeshua to be their Deliverer and Lord, Paul was calling the Philippians to accept a provocative claim that would run counter to the Roman authority and system that declared the emperor a god and political savior (Dobson 1511). In embracing Yeshua as Messiah, the Philippians were making a dangerous religious and political statement that could cost them their lives. As they embrace Yeshua faith and step out from their loyalty to their earthly citizenship, which included the emperor cult, Paul confirms the Philippians in their new heavenly citizenship with Yeshua as their Lord and Savior. Not only was Yeshua faith a religious decision for the Philippians but also a political decision (Rowland 239).

Paul called the Philippians to recognize that they were citizens of Heaven and despite the opposition they would face, their faith in Yeshua was worth the sacrifice. Life in Yeshua and citizenship in Heaven required rejection of their past pagan life and the syncretic religious life of Philippi for a new allegiance and an embracing of the Jewish God, Jewish Messiah, and Jewish Scriptures. They are redeemed Gentiles living for now in a pagan world but whose ultimate destiny and current citizenship is not of this world (Keown Vol. 1 55).

---

21 He will change the bodies we have in this humble state and make them like his glorious body, using the power which enables him to bring everything under his control.

The heavenly citizenship in verse 20 will require new spiritual bodies as the followers of Yeshua enter their new lives in their new home; they will be transformed into a spiritual body like that of the risen Yeshua (Fredriksen *Jesus* 59). Paul here used Yeshua as his model for the new life that is coming to those who are in Yeshua (Keener 560). In verse 21, we can see Paul giving a word of encouragement to the believers in Philippi that the hope in Messiah goes on into eternity as they, like the Messiah, will receive new, glorified bodies. Paul here is sharing with the Philippians this hope based on his own experience seeing the risen and glorified Yeshua on the Damascus Road in Acts 9 (Hurtado *One* 124).

Paul makes clear to the Philippians that the same resurrected, new body that Yeshua assumed at his resurrection is the hope for those who have put their faith in him. It is the power of the resurrection that guarantees not only their resurrection to eternal life but also the final vindication of the righteous and subjugation of the created order under the righteous rule of King Messiah. Thus, we see another glimpse of the lordship of Yeshua and Paul's understanding of Yeshua as one with the One God of Israel, another example of Paul's high Christology in the letter (Bockmuehl 236).

PHILIPPIANS 4

Don't worry about anything; on the contrary, make your requests known to God by prayer and petition, with thanksgiving.

—Philippians 4:6

Chapter Introduction

Philippians 4 is the final chapter of the letter in which Paul addresses the letter's underlying purpose: the issue of division among two leaders in the community. Throughout the letter Paul stresses that disunity is grounded in a lack of humility. Here Paul calls these leaders to return to unity grounded in their modeling of Yeshua's example.

This chapter also includes familiar verses on joyful living as a follower of Yeshua (verse 6); focusing on good things and rejecting evil thoughts (verse 8); and divine empowerment for works of service to God (verse 13).

Paul concludes the letter with gratitude to the Philippians for their faithful, financial, and physical support of his ministry (verses 14–18) and with words of encouragement and blessing. Indeed, Paul's beloved community of Philippi encouraged him also at the inception of his work spreading the Good News of Messiah throughout Europe and to the "ends of the earth" (Acts 1:8) in the first century of the Common Era.

Commentary

Closing Words (4:1)

---

1 So, my brothers, whom I love and long for, my joy and my crown, my dear friends, keep standing firm in union with the Lord.

As the victor in athletic competitions would receive a prize, usually an olive branch wreath/crown, Paul considers his relationship and ministry to the Philippians to be his prize for faithful service and a great source of joy in his final days (Ware 274).

Paul shares that the Philippians are a great joy to him, and despite his suffering and impending execution, he can rejoice that their faith in Yeshua and their growing more like the Messiah is a spiritual reward, a "crown" for their and his faithfulness to God.

Disunity in the Community (4:2–3)

---

2 I beg Evodia and I beg Syntyche to agree with each other in union with the Lord.

As Paul concludes the letter, he mentions the possible, primary reason for the letter: confronting the disunity in the community because of the disagreement between Evodia and Syntyche, two women in leadership among the Yeshua believers in Philippi. Paul knew conflicts among the leaders would be detrimental to the community and therefore, he took the opportunity in this letter to confront division between two prominent women in Philippi.

Paul's use of παρακαλεῖν (*parakaleo*), meaning "beg, urge, exhort, appeal to," shows the importance of this issue to him and the negative effect on the whole community with these two leaders being in disunity (Hawthorne 240).

Throughout the letter Paul has been dealing with the importance of humility with positive examples of himself in Chapter 1; the ultimate example of humility, Yeshua the Messiah, in Chapter 2; Timothy and Epaphroditus also in Chapter 2; and contrasting negative examples in Chapter 3. Given Paul's emphasis earlier in the letter on humility leading to unity, Paul sheds light on the issue of pride and a lack of humility in the relationship of Evodia and Syntyche, which not only affected them but was also an issue of concern for the whole Philippian Messianic Community.

Paul twice used the Greek word φρονέω (*phroneō*), which means "referring specifically to the attitude of people to one another." Paul first used *phroneō* to describe Yeshua's humble mindset in Philippians 2:5. Paul then used it here in imploring Evodia and Syntyche to unity for the sake of the community (Arndt *Lexicon* 26.16). Paul is reminding these women what their mindset should be (that of Messiah) and calling them to put aside their wrong attitude in order to model Yeshua, who is their ultimate example.

Unity in Philippi and within any Messianic community required the people to follow the example of Yeshua and model his self-sacrificing humility. Such behavior was particularly important for leaders such as Evodia and Syntyche, who were in a position of influence in their community. As Paul modeled Messiah, he expected those in leadership to do the same.

3 I request you, loyal Syzygus, to help these women; for they have worked hard proclaiming the Good News with me, along with Clement and the rest of my fellow-workers whose names are in the Book of Life.

Paul here appeals to Syzygus (a proper name in David H. Stern's translation) to help bring unity to the Philippian community by assisting Evodia and Syntyche to resolve the issue that divides them. (Interestingly, some translations do not use "Syzygus" as a proper name; for example, the English Standard Version (ESV) uses the word "companion," the English translation of the Greek *syzygus* (σύζυγος) for the person Paul calls to counsel the two women.)

Paul referred to Evodia and Syntyche as his "fellow-workers," a reference to their close working relationship with Paul in ministry (Reumann 610). Like Paul, they would have faced persecution for their commitment to the work of spreading the Good News of Messiah (Cohn-Sherbok 162).

As leaders in the community, their lack of unity affects the whole community. Throughout his letter Paul calls the Philippians to unity through modeling the humility of Yeshua, and as he closes the letter, he calls for unity and humility to begin among the leaders of the community (especially between Evodia and Syntyche), as they, like Paul, serve as examples for the people (Thielman 363).

In addressing the conflict between these two women leaders, Paul stresses the importance of accountability for all in the Philippian Messianic Community, from the leaders to everyone. (Barry, Phil. 4:2). Paul's emphasis on the importance of leaders serving as examples of Messiah is a theme throughout the letter. Just as Paul uses himself, Timothy, Epaphroditus, and Clement as examples, he also wants Evodia and Syntyche to resolve their disunity so they can be examples of Messiah to those people over which they have influence.

In his opening words of the letter (1:1), Paul addressed the congregational leaders and *shammashim* (deacons), clarifying that Philippi had an established leadership structure and making sure that the Philippian Messianic Community leaders were listening to his message. As the leaders of the community model the Messiah, their examples should draw the people to follow the example of Yeshua. Paul places great importance on the unity and Messiah-like modeling of leaders, and he makes clear his intent to bring Evodia and Syntyche back together as one in Messiah for their own sake as well as the betterment of the community.

Since the Philippians highly valued their Roman citizenship and the prominence of Philippi as a Roman colony, Paul declares that through their faith in Yeshua they have even greater citizenship as one written in the "Book of Life," a citizen of Heaven (Hawthorne 243). We can see this in Isaiah's prophetic words about the End of Days:

> Those left in Tziyon and remaining in Yerushalayim will
> be called holy and everyone in Yerushalayim written
> down for life. (Isa. 4:3)

The "Book of Life" is a Jewish concept that plays a prominent role in the final judgment described in the book of Revelation (20:12b) and also in the High Holy Day liturgy of *Rosh Hashanah* (Kasdan *God's Appointed Times* in Rubin 1692).

Living in Union with Messiah (4:4–6)

4 Rejoice in union with the Lord always! I will say it again: rejoice!

Here Paul calls the Philippians in this famous verse to rejoice, not as a temporary feeling or emotion but as a joy that has staying power based on their faith commitment to Yeshua (Stern *Commentary* 601). This joy is not just an emotion but an authentic experience of God's faithfulness and his continued promise of guidance, provision, protection, and direction (Juster 64).

The cause for the Philippians' rejoicing is the Good News that the Messiah will soon return and then they, along with all the redeemed, will enter the Messianic Kingdom and the new life forever with Yeshua. This assurance of death's defeat guarantees the righteous, eternal reign of Messiah would begin (Fredriksen *Jesus* 205–206).

5 Let everyone see how reasonable and gentle you are. The Lord is near!
6 Don't worry about anything; on the contrary, make your requests known to God by prayer and petition, with thanksgiving.

In memorable verse 6 Paul here is teaching the Philippians about the importance of prayer as a source of breaking from worry. The greatest counter to worrying is to place all concerns on God in prayer. David H. Stern made an interesting point that those who do not want to bring issues to God in prayer are showing pride in their unwillingness to release issues to God (*Commentary* 602). Again we see Paul teaching about humility, in this case by humbly bringing all issues to God in prayer. The greatest act of humility is to lay all one's needs before God, knowing that he is the source of life and the true Lord and King.

It is in this time of supplicatory prayer the Philippians can bring their most heartfelt needs and concerns before God. Simple supplicatory prayers like the ones Paul is recommending to the Philippians would later be integrated into the daily Jewish liturgy of the *Tachanun* prayers (Donin 202).

Call to Stand Firm in Their Faith (4:7-9)

7 Then God's shalom, passing all understanding, will keep your hearts and minds safe in union with the Messiah Yeshua. **8** In conclusion, brothers, focus your thoughts on what is true, noble, righteous, pure, lovable or admirable, on some virtue or on something praiseworthy.

Here are two more familiar, memorable verses. Paul encourages the Philippians to focus their thoughts on positive things as a way of living in a world that focuses on negative things and lacks truth, nobility, righteousness, and purity. Paul urges the Philippians to live in a broken world by focusing on that which is pure and unbroken since a mind focused on what is right will help the believer live within a lost world and not join in the lostness (Stern *Commentary* 602).

As God called the Jewish People to be holy (Lev. 20:26) and model the holiness of God, Paul offers the Philippians a practical way of holy living by focusing their minds on virtuous and pure things so they can live outwardly with hearts turned inward to that which is true and pure (Juster 75).

---

9 Keep doing what you have learned and received from me, what you have heard and seen me doing; then the God who gives shalom will be with you.

Paul encourages the Philippians to follow his example as a follower of Yeshua. Understanding that life going forward is the life of one "crucified with Messiah," Paul models Messiah in a life conformed to service of the crucified Yeshua (Furnish 6). Paul taught the Philippians by both his words in the letter and also in the life he led before them as a slave of Messiah Yeshua. He urges them to be encouraged and challenged by his example. As he modeled Messiah, they, too, should conform their lives to Messiah. The reward for this lifestyle is *shalom* (peace) in a fallen world where war and strife are ever present. Such peace comes by modeling Messiah and living distinctly in a world that calls for conformity.

Love and Thankfulness for the Philippians (4:10–18)

10 In union with the Lord I greatly rejoice that now, after this long time, you have let your concern for me express itself again. Of course, you were concerned for me all along, but you had no opportunity to express it. **11** Not that I am saying this to call attention to any need of mine; since, as far as I am concerned, I have learned to be content regardless of circumstances. **12** I know what it is to be in want, and I know what it is to have more than enough—in everything and in every way I have learned the secret of being full and being hungry, of having abundance and being in need.

These verses show the deep mutual love that Paul shared with the Philippians. As he gave his all to them in bringing the message of Messiah and cared for them as their shepherd from prison, they, too, showed their love in financial giving and in sending Epaphroditus to be their emissary to Paul in prison.

Paul teaches them a powerful lesson of living and being content in all circumstances. He clarifies he is not needing or requesting anything else from the Philippians.

13 I can do all things through him who gives me power.

In this famous verse Paul expresses complete trust in Yeshua for his needs and also for the empowerment to do his work of ministry. Paul's trust is secure in that the power to "do all things" does not rest on him but is found in the faithfulness of God, made known to him in Messiah Yeshua (Stern *Modern* 273).

From his own experience, Paul encourages the Yeshua-followers in Philippi to tap into divine power for their service to God and the Messianic Community. There is empowerment for service, not a blanket promise of divine power for all aspects of life or for all pursuits, but specifically divine power for service to God and for making the Messiah known in the world (Decker 426).

Paul here assures the Philippians of divine empowerment for good works and the spread of the Good News. We can see Paul echoing Yeshua's promise to his *talmidim* of divine empowerment for those walking in God's ways and observing the teachings of Yeshua:

> "If you love me, you will keep my commands; and I will ask the Father, and he will give you another comforting Counselor like me, the Spirit of Truth, to be with you forever. The world cannot receive him, because it neither sees nor knows him. You know him, because he is staying with you and will be united with you." (John 14:15–17)

Just as Yeshua promised the Holy Spirit to those who observed his commands and walked in his example, Paul can confidently commend to the Philippians the assurance of Holy Spirit empowerment as they serve Yeshua.

---

14 Nevertheless, it was good of you to share in my trouble.

Paul shares how the love that he has for the Philippians was grounded in their faithfulness to him, especially in his own time of need. In addition to the financial gifts that they sent him, which he will mention in the upcoming verses, the

Philippians also sent Epaphroditus to serve him in prison and they supported him through prayer. In short, Paul is deeply grateful to the Philippians for their support.

---

15 And you Philippians yourselves know that in the early days of my work spreading the Good News, when I left Macedonia, not a single congregation shared with me in the matter of giving and receiving—only you.

Paul refers to his work in Macedonia as the "early days" of his ministry even though he had started earlier to bring the Good News to Asia Minor. In Macedonia, Paul's mission to the Gentiles began in greater measure as his work was to mostly Gentile-majority cities. They could see his Apostleship to the Gentiles to have started in force in Philippi and here he acknowledged his thankfulness to the Philippians for launching his new work of bringing the Jewish Messiah to the Gentile world (Bockmuehl 1).

Though Paul taught in 1 Corinthians 9:6–14 that he and others involved in proclaiming the Good News of Yeshua should get their income from those to whom they minister, Paul did not seek financial support from the congregations he started and guided as a shepherd. With the Philippians, he made an exception grounded in their love for him and his love for them (MacArthur 306). Paul was mindful to avoid a patron-client relationship with his donors (Taylor 61), which would have hindered him from being independent to seek new opportunities for service.

16 Indeed, in Thessalonica when I needed it, you sent me aid twice.

17 I am not seeking the gift; rather, I am looking for what will increase the credit balance of your account.

Paul communicates to the Philippians that the real importance of their giving to him is not solely for meeting his financial needs but that in their giving, they were investing in his work and by so doing bearing fruit in their lives as a demonstration of their faith and commitment to the Messiah (Rosscup 64).

18 I have been more than paid in full: I have been filled since I have received from Epaphroditus the gifts you sent—they are a fragrant aroma, an acceptable sacrifice, one that pleases God well.

Thanking the Philippians for their gifts, Paul here makes a biblical analogy (from Leviticus 1–4) citing the "fragrant aroma" of the burnt offerings of the *Torah* (Dobson 1514). By referring to the gifts from the Philippians as gifts offered to God, Paul is distancing himself from being in debt to the Philippians. Also by calling their gifts a sacrifice to God, Paul can hold fast to his commitment to not preach the Gospel for his gain as he shared in his letter to the Thessalonians:

> For you yourselves know how you must imitate us, that
> we were not idle when we were among you. We did not
> accept anyone's food without paying; on the contrary, we
> labored and toiled, day and night, working so as not to

be a burden to any of you. It was not that we hadn't the right to be supported, but so that we could make ourselves an example to imitate. For even when we were with you, we gave you this command: if someone won't work, he shouldn't eat! (2 Thess. 3:7–10)

As Paul commends the Philippians for their lives of service to him and Messiah Yeshua, he clarifies that their devotion has matured to be an acceptable offering to God. Paul here uses language from the *Torah* (Exodus 29:18) to show that their giving to him was a sacrificial offering to God (Keener 566). Their willingness to give to Paul proved that they have learned well and are now imitating Yeshua in their daily lives (Rowland 259). In much the same way as later Rabbinic teaching would substitute prayer and mitzvot for the Temple sacrifice, Paul here imputes sacrificial status to the work of the Philippians on his behalf (Cyprian 456).

Words of Blessing and Encouragement (4:19–23)

19 Moreover, my God will fill every need of yours according to his glorious wealth, in union with the Messiah Yeshua.

Having spoken about how the Philippian community had met his needs, Paul here conveys the reassurance that God will provide for their needs. His confidence comes from the riches in the glory of Messiah Yeshua.

20 And to God our Father be the glory forever and ever. Amen.
21 Greet each of God's people in the Messiah Yeshua. The brothers with me send their greetings to you.

Paul concludes the letter with words of blessing giving honor to God the Father and a call to greet one another in the name of Messiah Yeshua. He also shares that the followers of Yeshua in Rome send greetings to their brothers and sisters in the faith in Philippi.

---

22 All God's people send greetings, but especially those in the Emperor's household.

For those who hold that Paul wrote the letter in Rome, this verse mentions members of the Emperor's household (in Rome), which can bolster their assertion (Stern *Commentary* 602)

---

23 The grace of the Lord Yeshua the Messiah be with your spirit.

Paul concluded the letter with a final word of blessing referencing the grace of the Lord Yeshua the Messiah as the seal of their faith and hope in which they live.

GLOSSARY

B.C.E/C.E.—The abbreviations B.C.E. and C.E., which mean "Before the Common Era" and "Common Era," are commonly used among scholars and within the Jewish community, instead of the more common B.C. ("Before Christ") and A.D. ("Anno Domini," which is Latin for "in the year of our Lord").

Jerusalem Council—An early guiding body that convened around 50/51 C.E. made up of the Apostles (Emissaries), Elders, and other prominent figures within the Yeshua-believing community. The purpose of the council, according to Acts 15 and Galatians 2, was to decide whether or not Gentiles must convert to Judaism and, therefore, be obligated to observe all the commandments of the Torah before becoming part of the Messianic Community. The final decision, after much debate, was that Gentiles are not required to convert to Judaism and therefore, are not obligated to keep most of the commandments. However, they did retain the prohibitions against idolatry, fornication, eating blood, and meat not properly slaughtered (i.e. "strangled," in most English versions) (see Acts 15:10–11 and 19–29).

One God of Israel— *ADONAI*, literally, "My Lord," a Hebrew word used by Jews to represent the Tetragrammaton, the sacred name of God consisting of the four Hebrew letters, Yud-Hey-Vav-Hey; but usually as LORD (all capital letters in many Bibles).

Septuagint—Commonly abbreviated as simply LXX, it is the earliest Greek translation of the *Tanakh*.

Tanakh—Jews refer to their Scriptures as the *Tanakh* (תנ״ך), which is an acronym for the three primary sections of the *Tanakh*—the *Torah* (Pentateuch) or the first five books of the Bible, *Nevi'im* (Prophets) and *K'tuvim* (Writings). The canon of the Christian Old Testament includes the same books as the Jewish canon but they are arranged in a different order.

Torah—The word literally means "teaching" or "instruction." It specifically refers to the first five books of the Bible—Genesis, Exodus, Leviticus, Numbers, and Deuteronomy. However, it can also be used to refer to Jewish teaching more generally.

Ya'akov—The original Hebrew form of the names Jacob and James, the brother of

Yeshua and early leader of the Messianic Jewish Community in Jerusalem.

Yeshua—The earliest followers of Jesus knew him by his original Hebrew name Yeshua (ישוע), the masculine form of the word for salvation/redemption, ישועה.

BIBLIOGRAPHY

Anders, Max. Galatians-Colossians. Vol. 8. Holman New Testament Commentary. Nashville, TN: Broadman & Holman Publishers, 1999.

Arndt, William, Frederick W. Danker, Walter Bauer, and F. Wilbur Gingrich. A Greek-English Lexicon of the New Testament and Other Early Christian Literature. Chicago: University of Chicago Press, 2000.

Arnold, Clinton E., ed. Zondervan Illustrated Bible Backgrounds Commentary. Grand Rapids: Zondervan, 2002.

Ash, Anthony Lee. Philippians, Colossians & Philemon. The College Press NIV Commentary. Joplin, MO: College Press, 1994.

Attridge, Harold W. and Wayne A. Meeks, eds. The HarperCollins Study Bible New Revised Standard Version, with the Apocryphal/Deuterocanonical books, fully rev. and updated; student ed. San Francisco: HarperSanFrancisco, 2006.

Aymer, Margaret P., Cynthia B. Kittredge and David A. Sánchez, eds. The Letters and Legacy of Paul. Lanham: Fortress Press, 2016.

Bahnsen, Greg L. , Commentary. The Theonomic Reformed Approach to Law and Gospel in Five Views on Law and Gospel (Counterpoints: Bible and Theology). Zondervan. Kindle Edition, 2010.

Barry, John D. et al. Faithlife Study Bible. Bellingham, WA: Lexham Press. 2012 2016.

Barry, John D., David Bomar, Derek R. Brown, Rachel Klippenstein, Douglas Mangum, Carrie Sinclair Wolcott, Lazarus Wentz, Elliot Ritzema, and Wendy Widder, eds. The Lexham Bible Dictionary. Bellingham, WA: Lexham Press, 2016.

Bateman IV, Herbert. "Were the Opponents at Philippi Necessarily Jewish?," – Bibliotheca Sacra 155, no. 617 (Jan), WORDsearch CROSS e-book, 1998.

Bates, Matthew W. Salvation by Allegiance Alone: Rethinking Faith, Works, and the Gospel of Jesus the King. Grand Rapids, MI: Baker Academic, a Division of Baker Publishing Group, 2017.

Berlin, Adele, Marc Zvi Brettler, and Michael Fishbane, eds. The Jewish Study Bible. New York: Oxford University Press, 2004.

Betz, Hans D. "Paul (Person)." In The Anchor Yale Bible Dictionary. Editor David N. Freedman. New York: Doubleday, 1992.

Boa, Kenneth. Conformed to His Image: Biblical and Practical Approaches to Spiritual Formation. Grand Rapids, MI: Zondervan, 2001.

Boccaccini, Gabriele, and Carlos A. Segovia. Paul the Jew: Rereading the Apostle as a Figure of Second Temple Judaism. Minneapolis: Fortress Press, 2016.

Bockmuehl, Markus. The Epistle to the Philippians. London: Continuum, 1997.

Boyarin, Daniel. The Jewish Gospels the Story of the Jewish Christ. New York: New Press, 2013.

Brannan, Rick, Ken M. Penner, Israel Loken, Michael Aubrey, and Isaiah Hoogendyk, eds. The Lexham English Septuagint. Bellingham, WA: Lexham Press, 2012.

Brown, Paul S. "The Heavenly Mindset –Maintaining Unity in the Body" Part Three". Sermon Notes, The Bridge Bible Fellowship, Reseda, CA, December 16 2007.

———. "The Heavenly Mindset –Maintaining Unity in the Body" Part Four". Sermon Notes, The Bridge Bible Fellowship, Reseda, CA, January 6 2008.

Brumbach, Joshua. Jude: Faith and the Destructive Influence of Heresy. A Messianic Commentary. Clarksville, MD: Messianic Jewish Publishers, 2014.

Campbell, Douglas A. The Deliverance of God: An Apocalyptic Rereading of Justification in Paul. Grand Rapids, MI; Cambridge, U.K.: William B. Eerdmans Publishing Company, 2013.

Capes, David B. "YHWH Texts and Monotheism in Paul's Christology." In Early Jewish and Christian Monotheism. London; New York: T&T Clark, 2004.

Carson, D. A. and Douglas J. Moo. An Introduction to the New Testament, Second Edition. Grand Rapids, MI: Zondervan, 2005.

Chandler, Matt, and Jared C. Wilson. To Live Is Christ, To Die Is Gain. Colorado Springs, CO: David C Cook, 2013.

Charles, Robert Henry, ed., Pseudepigrapha of the Old Testament, vol. 2. Oxford: Clarendon Press, 1913.

Chrysostom, John. "Homilies of St. John Chrysostom, Archbishop of Constantinople, on the Epistle of St. Paul the Apostle to the Philippians." In Saint Chrysostom: Homilies on Galatians, Ephesians, Philippians, Colossians, Thessalonians, Timothy, Titus, and Philemon, edited by Philip Schaff, translated by W. C. Cotton and John Albert Broadus 13:230. A Select Library of the Nicene and Post-Nicene Fathers of the Christian Church, First Series. New York: Christian Literature Company, 1889.

Cohn-Sherbok, Dan. Voices of Messianic Judaism: Confronting Critical Issues Facing a Maturing Movement. Baltimore, MD: Messianic Jewish Publishers, 2001.

Couch, James F., ed. Philippians Running the Race. Nashville, Tenn: Serendipity House, 2003.

Cousar, Charles B. Philippians and Philemon A Commentary. Louisville, Kentucky, 2013.

Coxe, A. Cleveland. The Ante-Nicene Fathers. vol. 1. Buffalo, NY: Christian Literature Company, 1885.

Culpepper, R. "Paul's Mission to the Gentile World: Acts 13-19," – Review and Expositor 071, no. 4 (Fall), WORDsearch CROSS e-book, 1974.

Cyprian of Carthage. "On the Lord's Prayer." In Fathers of the Third Century: Hippolytus, Cyprian, Novatian, Appendix, edited by Alexander Roberts, James Donaldson, and A. Cleveland Coxe, translated by Robert Ernest Wallis 5:456. The Ante-Nicene Fathers. Buffalo, NY: Christian Literature Company, 1886.

Das, A. Andrew. Paul and the Stories of Israel: Grand Thematic Narratives in Galatians. Minneapolis: Fortress Press, 2016.

Decker, Rodney J. "An Evaluation of the 2011 Edition of the New International Version." Themelios 36, no. 3, 2011.

Deissmann, G. A. Bible Studies: Contributions chiefly from papyri and inscriptions to the history of the language, the literature and the religion of Hellenistic Judaism and primitive Christianity. Edinburgh: T & T Clark, 1901.

Dobson, Kent. NIV First-Century Study Bible Explore Scripture in Its Jewish and Early Christian Context (Notes). Grand Rapids, Mich: Zondervan, 2014.

Donin, Hayim H. To Pray as a Jew: A Guide to the Prayer Book and the Synagogue Service. S.l.: Basic Books. Kindle, 1991.

Dunn, James D. The Theology of Paul the Apostle. Grand Rapids, Mich: Eerdmans, 2003.

Edwards, Mark Julian, and Thomas Clark Oden. Ancient Christian Commentary: Galatians, Ephesians, Philippians. Downers Grove, IL: InterVarsity Press, 2014.

Ehrensperger, Kathy. That We May Be Mutually Encouraged : Feminism and the New Perspective in Pauline Studies. London; New York: T&T Clark. 2004.

Eisenberg, Joyce, and Ellen Scolnic. Dictionary of Jewish Words: A JPS Guide. Jewish Publication Society, 2006.

Elwell, Walter A., and Barry J. Beitzel. "Book of Life." Baker Encyclopedia of the Bible. Grand Rapids, MI: Baker Book House, 1988.

Emslie, Robert S. Jewish Messianic Expectations in Intertestamental Jewish Writings and the Messianic Revelation in the Person of Jesus of Nazareth. Academia.edu - Share Research. Last modified May 21 2014. https://www.academia.edu/15155980/ Jewish_Messianic_Expectations_in_Intertestamental_ Jewish_Writings_and_the_Messianic_Revelation_in_the_ Person_of_Jesus_of_Nazareth, 2014.

Fee, Gordon D. Paul's Letter to the Philippians. Grand Rapids, MI: Wm.B. Eerdmans Publishing Co., 1995.

————. Pauline Christology: An Exegetical-Theological Study. Peabody, MA: Hendrickson Publishers, 2007.

Florentino, García Martínez and Eibert J. C. Tigchelaar "The Dead Sea Scrolls Study Edition (translations)." Leiden; New York: Brill, 1997-1998.

Fredriksen, Paula. From Jesus to Christ the Origins of the New Testament Images of Jesus. Cumberland: Yale University Press, 2014.

————. "The Question of Worship: Gods, Pagans, and the Redemption of Israel." In Paul within Judaism: Restoring the First-Century Context to the Apostle, edited by Mark D. Nanos and Magnus Zetterholm. Minneapolis, MN: Fortress Press, 2015.

———. Paul: The Pagans' Apostle. New Haven, CT: Yale University Press, 2017.

Friedman, David. They Loved the Torah: What Yeshua's First Followers Really Thought about the Law. Baltimore, MD: Messianic Jewish Publishers, 2001.

———. At the Feet of Rabbi Gamaliel: Rabbinic Influence in Paul's Teachings, Clarksville, MD: Lederer Books: A division of Messianic Jewish Publishers, 2013.

Friesen, Ivan D. Isaiah. Scottdale, PA; Waterloo, ON: Herald Press, 2009.

Furnish, Victor Paul. "On Putting Paul in His Place." Journal of Biblical Literature 113, 1994.

Giglio, Louie, Max Lucado, John Piper, Ravi K. Zacharias, and Randy C. Alcorn. The Jesus Bible: Sixty-six Books. One Story. All about One Name. Grand Rapids, MI: Published by Zondervan, 2016.

Grenz, Stanley. Theology for the Community of God. Grand Rapids, Mich: Eerdmans, 2000.

Gromacki, Robert. Twenty-First Century Biblical Commentary Series – The Books of Philippians and Colossians: Joy and Completeness in Christ, ed. Mal Couch and Ed Hindson. Chattanooga, TN: AMG Publishers. WORDsearch CROSS e-book, 2003.

Hamm, Dennis. Philippians, Colossians, Philemon. Edited by Peter S. Williamson and Mary Healy. Catholic Commentary on Sacred Scripture. Grand Rapids, MI: Baker Academic, 2013.

Hansen, G. W. The Letter to the Philippians: Pillar New Testament Commentary [PNTC]. Grand Rapids, Mich: William B. Eerdmans Pub. Co., 2009.

Hanson, Anthony Tyrrell. The Pioneer Ministry; the Relation of Church and Ministry. London: SCM, 1961.

Harlow, Daniel C. "Early Judaism and Early Christianity." Edited by John J. Collins. The Eerdmans Dictionary of Early Judaism. Grand Rapids, MI; Cambridge, U.K.: William B. Eerdmans Publishing Company, 2010.

Hartog, Paul A. "Macedonia." Edited by John D. Barry, David Bomar, Derek R. Brown, Rachel Klippenstein, Douglas Mangum, Carrie Sinclair Wolcott, Lazarus Wentz, Elliot Ritzema, and Wendy Widder. The Lexham Bible Dictionary. Bellingham, WA: Lexham Press, 2016.

Hawthorne, Gerald F. Philippians. Vol. 43. Word Biblical Commentary. Dallas: Word, Incorporated, 2004.

Holy Bible: English Standard Version. Wheaton, IL: Crossway Bibles, 2001.

Holy Bible: Revised Standard Version. London, 1952.

Horner, Barry E., and E. Ray. Clendenen. Future Israel: Why Christian Anti-Judaism Must Be Challenged. Nashville, TN: B & H Academic, 2007.

Horsley, Richard A. Paul and Empire: Religion and Power in Roman Imperial Society. Harrisburg, PA: Trinity Press International, 2006.

Huckel, Tom. The Rabbinic Messiah. Philadelphia, PA: Hananeel House. 1998.

Hughes, R. Kent. Philippians: The Fellowship of the Gospel. Preaching the Word. Wheaton, IL: Crossway Books, 2007.

Hurtado, Larry W. How on Earth Did Jesus Become a God?: Historical Questions about Earliest Devotion to Jesus. Grand Rapids, MI; Cambridge, U.K.: William B. Eerdmans Publishing Company, 2005.

————. One God, One Lord: Early Christian Devotion and Ancient Jewish Monotheism. London: Bloomsbury, 2015.

Juster, Daniel C. Growing to Maturity: A Messianic Jewish Discipleship Guide. Clarksville, MD: Lederer Books/ Messianic Jewish Publishers, 2011.

Kärkkäinen, Veli-Matti. Christian Understandings of the Trinity: The Historical Trajectory. Minneapolis, MN: Fortress Press, 2017.

Kasdan, Barney. God's Appointed Times: A Practical Guide for Understanding and Celebrating the Biblical Holidays. 2nd ed. Clarksville, MD: Messianic Jewish Publishers, 2007.

Keener, Craig S. The IVP Bible Background Commentary: New Testament 2nd Ed. Downers Grove, IL: InterVarsity Press, 2014.

Keown, Mark J. Philippians. Edited by H. Wayne House, W. Hall Harris III, and Andrew W. Pitts. vol. 1. Evangelical Exegetical Commentary. Bellingham, WA: Lexham Press, 2017.

Kinzer, Mark S. Postmissionary Messianic Judaism Redefining Christian Engagement with the Jewish People. Grand Rapids: Baker Publishing Group, 2005.

Lang, Friedrich. "Σκύβαλον." Edited by Gerhard Kittel, Geoffrey W. Bromiley, and Gerhard Friedrich. Theological Dictionary of the New Testament. Grand Rapids, MI: Eerdmans, 1964–.

Lauterbach, Jacob Zallel. Mekilta de-Rabbi Ishmael. New ed. Philadelphia, Pa: Jewish Publication Society, 2004.

Leman, Derek. Divine Messiah. Atlanta, GA: Mount Olive Press, 2014.

Lieu, Judith M. Neither Jew nor Greek? Constructing Early Christianity. London; New York: T&T Clark, 2002.

Lightfoot, Joseph Barber, ed. Saint Paul's Epistle to the Philippians. Classic Commentaries on the Greek New Testament. London: Macmillan and Co., ltd., 1913.

———. Philippians. Crossway Classic Commentaries. Wheaton, IL: Crossway Books, 1994.

Lightfoot, Joseph Barber, and J. R. Harmer. The Apostolic Fathers. London: Macmillan and Co., 1891.

Lightner, Robert P. "Philippians." In The Bible Knowledge Commentary: An Exposition of the Scriptures, edited by J. F. Walvoord and R. B. Zuck. Wheaton, IL: Victor Books, 1985.

Lockyer, Herbert. All About God in Christ. Peabody, Mass: Hendrickson Publishers, 1995.

Loh, I-Jin, and Eugene Albert Nida. A Handbook on Paul's Letter to the Philippians. UBS Handbook Series. New York: United Bible Societies, 1995.

Lumbroso, Patrick Gabriel. Under the Fig Tree: Messianic Thought through the Hebrew Calendar. Clarksville, MD: Lederer Books A division of Messianic Jewish Publishers, 2010.

MacArthur, John. New Testament Commentary - Philippians. Chicago: Moody, 2001.

Mackintosh, H. R. The Doctrine of the Person of Christ. New York: Charles Scribner's and Sons, 1921.

MacLeod, David J. "The Exaltation of Christ: An Exposition of Philippians 2:9-11 ." Biblioteca Sacra: 158:632 (Oct 2001).

Malda, Barbara D., ed. Come and Worship: Ways to Worship from the Hebrew Scriptures. Clarksville, MD: Lederer Books/ Messianic Jewish Publishers, 2015.

Melick, Richard R. Philippians, Colossians, Philemon. Nashville: Broadman & Holman Publishers, 1991.

Merida, Tony, Francis Chan, David Platt, and Daniel L. Akin. Exalting Jesus in Philippians. Nashville, TN: Holman Reference, 2016.

Merkle, Benjamin L., Jason C. Meyer, Alistair I. Wilson, David W. Chapman, and Denny Burk. Ephesians–Philemon. Edited by Iain M. Duguid, James M. Hamilton Jr., and Jay Sklar. vol. XI. ESV Expository Commentary. Wheaton, IL: Crossway, 2018.

Miller, Jeffrey E. "Epaphroditus." Edited by John D. Barry, David Bomar, Derek R. Brown, Rachel Klippenstein, Douglas Mangum, Carrie Sinclair Wolcott, Lazarus Wentz, Elliot Ritzema, and Wendy Widder. The Lexham Bible Dictionary. Bellingham, WA: Lexham Press, 2016.

Moltmann, Jürgen. "Is God Incarnate in All That Is?" in Gregersen, N. H. Incarnation: On the Scope and Depth of Christology. Minneapolis, MN: Fortress Press, 2015.

Motyer, J.A. Message of Philippians—Jesus Our Joy. Inter-varsity Press, 1997.

Moule, C. F. D. "Further Reflections on Philippians," 2:5-11,» In Apostolic History and the Gospel: Biblical and Historical Essays Presented to F.F. Bruce. Exeter: The Paternoster Press, 1970.

Nadler, Sam. "How Can a Jew Believe in Jesus and Still Be Jewish?" Accessed February 13 2018. http://wordofmessiah. org/messianic-resources/messianic-answers-to- jewish-questions-sam-nadler/how-can-a-jew-believe-in-jesus-and-still-be- jewish%E2%80%8B-sam-nadler/.

Nanos, Mark. «A Jewish View by Mark Nanos.» In Four Views on the Apostle Paul, Nashville, Tenn: B & H Academic, 2012.

———. «Paul's Polemic in Philippians 3 as Jewish-Subgroup Vilification of Local Non-Jewish Cultic and Philosophical Alternatives.» Journal for the Study of Paul and His Letters 3. no. 1 (2013). http://www.jstor.org/stable/26426477.

———. Reading Corinthians and Philippians within Judaism: Collected Essays of Mark D. Nanos. Cascade, 2018.

Nanos, Mark D. and Magnus Zetterholm, eds. Paul within Judaism: Restoring the First- Century Context to the Apostle. Minneapolis, Minnesota: Fortress Press, 2015.

Neusner, Jacob. The Mishnah: A New Translation. New Haven, CT: Yale University Press, 1988.

———. Judaisms and Their Messiahs at the Turn of the Christian Era. Cambridge U.K.: Cambridge Univ. Press, 2003.

Neusner, Jacob, Alan J. Avery-Peck, and William Scott Green, eds. The Encyclopedia of Judaism. Leiden; Boston; Köln: Brill, 2000.

NIV Essentials Study Bible. Grand Rapids, MI: Zondervan, 2013.

Nolan, Albert. Jesus before Christianity 25 Anniversary ed. New York: Orbis Books, 2001.

Novenson, Matthew V. "The Jewish Messiahs, the Pauline Christ, and the Gentile Question." Journal of Biblical Literature. 128, no. 2 (2009): 357-73. doi:10.2307/25610187.

O'Brien, Peter Thomas. The Epistle to the Philippians: A Commentary on the Greek Text. Grand Rapids, MI: William B. Eerdmans Publishing Company, 2014.

O'Callaghan, Paul. God Ahead of Us: The Story of Divine Grace. Minneapolis: Fortress Press, 2014.

Oden, Thomas C. The Word of Life: Systematic Theology, vol. II. San Francisco, HarperSanFrancisco, 1992.

Pannenberg, Wolfhart, and Geoffrey William Bromiley. Systematic Theology. Grand Rapids, Mich.: Eerdmans, 1991.

Parsons, Mikeal C. "Appendices in the New Testament." Themelios 17, no. 2, 1992.

Pearson, Brook W. R. "CIVIC Cults." Dictionary of New Testament Background: A Compendium of Contemporary Biblical Scholarship. Downers Grove, IL: InterVarsity Press, 2000.

Polycarp of Smryna. "The Epistle of Polycarp to the Philippians." In The Apostolic Fathers with Justin Martyr and Irenaeus, edited by Alexander Roberts, James Donaldson, and A. Cleveland Coxe 1:33. The Ante-Nicene Fathers. Buffalo, NY: Christian Literature Company, 1885.

"Rashi on Genesis 1:4." Sefaria: A Living Library of Jewish Texts Online. Accessed December 21 2018. https://www.sefaria. org/Rashi_on_Genesis.1.4?lang=bi.

Redford, Doug. The New Testament Church: Acts-Revelation. vol. 2. Standard Reference Library: New Testament. Cincinnati, OH: Standard Pub, 2007.

Reed, Jeffrey T. "Philippians 3:1 and the Epistolary Hesitation Formulas: The Literary Integrity of Philippians, Again." Journal of Biblical Literature 115, 1996.

Rengstorf, Karl Heinrich. "Δοῦλος, Σύνδουλος, Δούλη, Δουλέυω, Δουλεία, Δουλόω, Καταδουλόω, Δουλαγωγέω, Ὀφθαλμοδουλία." Edited by Gerhard Kittel, Geoffrey W. Bromiley, and Gerhard Friedrich. Theological Dictionary of the New Testament. Grand Rapids, MI: Eerdmans, 1964.

Reumann, John. Philippians: A New Translation with Introduction and Commentary. Vol. 33B. Anchor Yale Bible. New Haven; London: Yale University Press, 2008.

Roberts, Alexander, James Donaldson and A. C. Coxe. The Apostolic Fathers with Justin Martyr and Irenaeus. Buffalo, NY: Christian Literature Company, 1885.

Robertson, A.T. Word Pictures in the New Testament. Nashville, TN: Broadman Press, 1933.

Rodríguez, Rafael, and Matthew Thiessen. The So-called Jew in Paul's Letter to the Romans. Minneapolis: Augsburg Fortress, 2016.

Rosscup, James. "Fruit in the New Testament." Bibliotheca Sacra 125, no. 497 (Jan) 1968.

Rowland, Christopher. Christian Origins an Account of the Setting and Character of the Most Important Messianic Sect of Judaism, 2nd ed. London: SPCK, 2002.

Rubin, Barry, Gen. Ed. The Complete Jewish Study Bible. Peabody, MA: Hendrickson Bibles/Messianic Jewish Publishers & Resources, 2016.

Sanders, E. P. Paul, the Law, and the Jewish People. Minneapolis, MN: Fortress Press, 1983.

———. Paul: The Apostle's Life, Letters, and Thought. Minneapolis, MN: Fortress Press, 2015.

Schäfer, Peter. Judeophobia: Attitudes toward the Jews in the Ancient World, Digital print ed. Cambridge (Mass.): Harvard University Press, 2014.

Schreiner, Thomas R. "Circumcision." Edited by Gerald F. Hawthorne, Ralph P. Martin, and Daniel G. Reid. Dictionary of Paul and His Letters. Downers Grove, IL: InterVarsity Press, 1993.

———. "Interpreting the Pauline Epistles." Southern Baptist Journal of Theology 03, no. 3 (Fall), WORDsearch CROSS e-book, 1999.

———. Commentary on Hebrews. Nashville, TN: B&H Publishing Group, 2015.

Shillington, V. G. James and Paul: The Politics of Identity at the Turn of the Ages. Minneapolis, MN: Fortress Press, 2015.

Silva, Moisés, ed. Philippians 2nd print ed. Grand Rapids, Mich: Baker Academic, 2007.

Singer, Isidore, ed. The Jewish Encyclopedia: A Descriptive Record of the History, Religion, Literature, and Customs of the Jewish People from the Earliest Times to the Present Day 12 volumes. New York; London: Funk & Wagnalls, 1901–1906.

Sloan, Robert B., Jr. NT344 Paul's Theology and the Letter to the Philippians. Logos Mobile Education. Bellingham, WA: Lexham Press, 2015.

Soulen, R. Kendall. "The Standard Canonical Narrative and the Problem of Supersessionism." In Introduction to Messianic Judaism. Grand Rapids, MI: Zondervan. Kindle eBook, 2013.

Sproul, R. C. R. The Unexpected Jesus: The Truth Behind His Biblical Names. Fearn, UK: Christian Focus Publications, 2005.

Spurgeon, Charles and Holman Bible Staff. CSB Spurgeon Study Bible. Nashville, Tennessee: Holman Bible Publishers. WORDsearch CROSS e-book, 2017.

Stern, David H. Complete Jewish Bible: An English Version of the Tanakh (Old Testament) and B'rit Hadashah (New Testament). 1st ed. Clarksville, MD: Jewish New Testament Publications, 1988.

———. Jewish New Testament Commentary: a Companion Volume to the Jewish New Testament. Clarksville, MD: Jewish New Testament Publications, 1992.

———. Messianic Judaism : A Modern Movement with an Ancient Past. Clarksville, MD: Messianic Jewish Publishers, 2007.

Stowers, Stanley K. "Friends and Enemies in the Politics of Heaven." In Pauline Theology, Vol. I: Thessalonians, Philippians, Galatians, Philemon. Edited by Jouette M. Bassler. Minneapolis: Fortress, 1994.

Stuckenbruck, Loren T. and Wendy E. North. Early Jewish and Christian Monotheism. London; New York: T&T Clark, 2004.

Tabletalk Magazine, July 2008: "The 8th Century." Lake Mary, FL: Ligonier Ministries, 2008.

Taylor, Walter F. Paul, Apostle to the Nations an Introduction. Minneapolis: Fortress Press, 2012.

The Jesus Bible Sixty-Six Books. One Story. All About One Name, New International Version. Zondervan Publishing House: Grand Rapids, Mich, 2016.

Thielman, Frank S. In Zondervan Illustrated Bible Backgrounds Commentary: Romans–Philemon. Edited by Clinton Arnold. Grand Rapids: Zondervan, 2002.

Vander Meulen, Elizabeth L., and Barbara D. Malda. His Names Are Wonderful: Getting to Know God through His Hebrew Names. Baltimore, MD: Messianic Jewish Publishers, 2005.

VanGemeren, Willem A. The Law is the Perfection of Righteousness in Jesus Christ: A Reformed Perspective in Five Views on Law and Gospel (Counterpoints: Bible and Theology). Zondervan. Kindle Edition, 1999.

Verhoef, Eduard. Philippi: How Christianity Began in Europe: The Epistle to the Philippians and the Excavations at Philippi. London; New York; New Delhi; Sydney: Bloomsbury, 2013.

Waddell, James A. The Messiah: A Comparative Study of the Enochic Son of Man and the Pauline Kyrios. Edited by James H. Charlesworth. vol. 10. Jewish and Christian Texts in Contexts and Related Studies Series. London; New York: T&T Clark, 2011.

Walvoord, John F. "Chapter III Israel and the Nations." From The Nations in Prophecy. Welcome | Walvoord.com. Accessed April 2, 2019. https://walvoord.com/article/294, 1967.

______. To Live Is Christ. Galaxie Software, 2007.

Ware, James P. Paul and the Mission of the Church: Philippians in Ancient Jewish Context. Grand Rapids, MI: Baker Academic, 2011.

Wright, Christopher J. H. Knowing Jesus through the Old Testament. Carlisle: Langham Preaching Resources, 2014.

Wright, N.T. "The Paul of History and the Apostle of Faith" Tyndale Bulletin 29, no. 1 (NA), WORDsearch CROSS e-book, 1978.

―――. The Resurrection of the Son of God. Christian Origins and the Question of God. London: Society for Promoting Christian Knowledge, 2003.

―――. New Testament for Everyone – Paul for Everyone: The Prison Letters: Ephesians, Philippians, Colossians and Philemon. Louisville, KY: Westminster John Knox Press, 2004.

Young, Brad H. Paul the Jewish Theologian: A Pharisee among Christians, Jews, and Gentiles. Grand Rapids, MI: Baker Academic, 2012.

Zuck, R. B. The Speaker's Quote Book: Over 4,500 Illustrations and Quotations for All Occasions. Grand Rapids, MI: Kregel Publications, 1997.

About the Author

R. Sean Emslie is a Messianic Jewish theologian and Bible teacher. He has been serving within the Messianic Jewish community since 1989, including service with Chosen People Ministries, the Messianic Jewish Theological Institute, and currently, Ahavat Zion Messianic Jewish Synagogue in the Los Angeles area. He is a life-long learner currently working on his third master's degree, an MA in Jewish Studies at Spertus Institute, in preparation for pursuing Spertus's Doctor of Science in Jewish Studies. He earned an MA in Christian Studies from Grand Canyon University, an MS in Education Technology from Full Sail University, and a BA in Religious Studies with a Jewish Studies focus from California State University, Northridge. He has also taken Jewish Studies courses at the Messianic Jewish Theological Institute, American Jewish University, and Netzer David Yeshiva.

OTHER RELATED RESOURCES

Available at Messianic Jewish Resources Int'l. • www.messianicjewish.net
1-800-410-7367
(Check our website for current discounts and promotions)

First Time in History!

General Editor: Rabbi Barry Rubin
Theological Editor: Dr. John Fischer

The Complete Jewish Study Bible
Insights for Jews and Christians
—Dr. David H. Stern

A One-of-a-Kind Study Bible that illuminates the Jewish background and context of God's word so it is more fully understandable. Uses the updated *Complete Jewish Bible* text by David H. Stern, including notes from the *Jewish New Testament Commentary* and contributions from Scholars listed below. 1990 pages.

Hardback	978-1619708679	$49.95
Flexisoft	978-1619708693	$79.95
Leather	978-1619708709	$139.95

< Hardcover Edition

Leather Edition w/color gift box   Flexisoft Edition w/color sleeve

 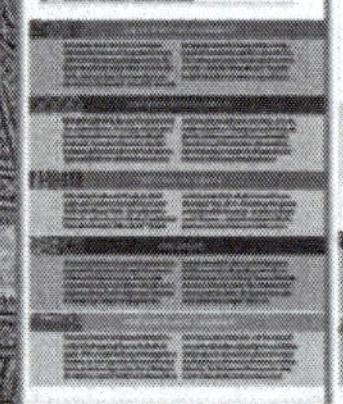 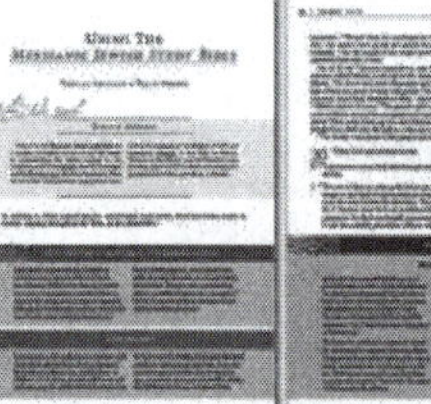

CONTRIBUTORS & SCHOLARS

Rabbi Dr. Glenn Blank	Forbes	Rabbi Barney Kasdan	Rosenberg
Dr. Michael Brown	Rabbi Dr. David	Dr. Craig S. Keener	Rabbi Isaac Roussel
Rabbi Steven Bernstein	Friedman	Rabbi Elliot Klayman	Dr. Michael Rydelnik
Rabbi Joshua	Dr. Arnold	Jordan Gayle Levy	Dr. Jeffrey Seif
Brumbach	Fruchtenbaum	Dr. Ronald Moseley	Rabbi Tzahi Shapira
Rabbi Ron Corbett	Dr. John Garr	Rabbi Dr. Rich Nichol	Dr. David H. Stern
Pastor Ralph Finley	Pastor David Harris	Rabbi Mark J. Rantz	Dr. Bruce Stokes
Rabbi Dr. John Fischer	Benjamin Juster	Rabbi Russ Resnik	Dr. Tom Tribelhorn
Dr. Patrice Fischer	Rabbi Dr. Daniel Juster	Dr. Richard Robinson	Dr. Forrest Weiland
Rebbitzen Malkah	Dr. Walter C. Kaiser	Rabbi Dr. Jacob	Dr. Marvin Wilson

QUOTES BY JEWISH SCHOLARS & SAGES

Dr. Daniel Boyarin
Dr. Amy-Jill Levine
Rabbi Jonathan Sacks
Rabbi Gamaliel
Rabbi Hillel
Rabbi Shammai
Rabbi Akiva
Maimonides
and many more

Complete Jewish Bible: *An English Version*
—Dr. David H. Stern (Available March 2017)

Now, the most widely used Messianic Jewish Bible around the world, has updated text with introductions added to each book, written from a biblically Jewish perspective. The CJB is a unified Jewish book, a version for Jews and non-Jews alike; to connect Jews with the Jewishness of the Messiah, and non-Jews with their Jewish roots. Names and terms are returned to their original Hebrew and presented in easy-to-understand transliterations, enabling the reader to say them the way *Yeshua* (Jesus) did! 1728 pages.

Paperback	978-1936716845	$29.95
Hardcover	978-1936716852	$34.95
Flexisoft Cover	978-1936716869	$49.95

Jewish New Testament
—Dr. David H. Stern

The New Testament is a Jewish book, written by Jews, initially for Jews. Its central figure was a Jew. His followers were all Jews; yet no other version really communicates its original, essential Jewishness. Uses neutral terms and Hebrew names. Highlights Jewish references and corrects mistranslations. Freshly translated into English from Greek, this is a must read to learn about first-century faith. 436 pages

Hardback	978-9653590069	**JB02**	$19.99
Paperback	978-9653590038	**JB01**	$14.99
Spanish	978-1936716272	**JB17**	$24.99

Also available in French, German, Polish, Portuguese and Russian.

Jewish New Testament Commentary
—Dr. David H. Stern

This companion to the *Jewish New Testament* enhances Bible study. Passages and expressions are explained in their original cultural context. 15 years of research. 960 pages.

Hardback	978-9653590083	**JB06**	$34.99
Paperback	978-9653590113	**JB10**	$29.99

Is Christ *Really* The "End of The Law"?
Another Look at *Telos* in Romans 10:4
—Drs. Jeffrey and Barri Cae Seif

"There are few Pauline statements more controversial than Romans 10:4, specifically the meaning of the word τέλος, telos.

τέλος γὰρ νόμου Χριστὸς εἰς δικαιοσύνην παντὶ τῷ πιστεύοντι.

The verse has traditionally been rendered, "For Christ is the *end* of the Law for righteousness to everyone who believes." Some say, "For the *goal* at which the Torah aims is the Messiah" while others prefer *new beginning*. Still others offer, "For Messiah is the *end* of the Torah, that everyone who has faith may be justified" or "Messiah is the *culmination* of the Torah so that there may be righteousness for everyone believes." 179 Pages

Paperback	978-1733935418	$21.99

Messianic Jewish Orthodoxy
The Essence of Our Faith, History and Best Practices
–Dr. Jeffrey Seif, General Editor

A work from the moderate, conservative center of the Messianic Jewish revival. This book speaks to the interests that group and the Church have in Jews, Israel and eschatology, with a need for a more-balanced consideration of faith, theology and practice—from Jewish perspectives.

This is vital for the many tens of thousands of Jews who have come to faith and who participate in Messianic Jewish experience and also those who frequent churches. Our non-Jewish friends who associate with the Messianic Jewish movement will find this book beneficial as well. It represents some of our best thinking and practice. 314 pages

Paperback	978-1733935425	$26.99

Demonstrating the Wonderful Power and Word of God in
The Life and Ministry of ELIJAH and ELISHA
—Dr. Walter C. Kaiser, Jr.

It's no wonder Old Testament professor Walt Kaiser is one of America's most beloved Bible expositors. This series of studies on Elijah and Elisha is vintage Kaiser, interspersed with his trademark humor. Organized in outline format, it offers an easy-to-follow look at the lives of two of the most famous and lively prophets ever to grace the pages of the Old Testament. Highly recommended to enhance anyone's study of the Scriptures! 208 pages

| Paperback | 978-1733935449 | $17.99 |

Social Justice The Bible and Application for Our Times
—Daniel C. Juster

In this work, addressing many of the social justice issues of today, one of the more seasoned Messianic Jewish leaders and scholars, Dr. Dan Juster, offers his thoughts. Not an academic book, we read what this well-known pioneer of Messianic Judaism, director of Tikkun International, founding president of the Union of Messianic Jewish Congregations and senior pastor of Beth Messiah Congregation from 1978-2012, thinks about the way our world is today. You will find his thoughts challenging and surprising. 124 pages

| Paperback | 978-1733935456 | $12.99 |

The Book of Ruth

This delightful version of *The Book of Ruth* includes the full text from the *Complete Jewish Bible* on the left page of the two-page spread. On the right are artful illustrations with brief story summaries that can be read to young children. Can be read any time during the year, but especially on *Shavuot* (Pentecost), the anniversary of the giving of the Torah on Mount Sinai and when the Holy Spirit was poured out on Yeshua's disciples (Acts 2). *The Book of Ruth* points to Yeshua as the ultimate Kinsman Redeemer.
6 x 9 inches, 26 pages with full color illustrations.

| Paperback | 978-1-936716-94-4 | $ 9.99 |

The Book of Esther

This delightful version of *The Book of Esther* includes the full text from the *Complete Jewish Bible* on the left page of the two-page spread. On the right are artful illustrations with brief story summaries that can be read to young children. Can be read any time during the year, but especially during *Purim*, the festival that celebrates how Queen Esther risked her life and became a vessel for the deliverance of her people Israel. Though God is not mentioned, Mordecai and Esther humbled themselves before God by fasting and praying, which showed dependence upon him. God answered and delivered his people while bringing the proud Haman to justice.
6 x 9 inches, 34 pages with full color illustrations.

| Paperback | 978-1-936716-95-1 | $ 9.99 |

Dear You
Letters of Identity in Yeshua ~ for Women ~
—Victoria Humphrey

Dear You is about discovering the truth of who you are as a beloved and courageous daughter of the King. It is an invitation to uncover what Elohim says about you through Scripture, silencing all other noise that vies to define you. While weaving together personal testimonies from other women, along with an opportunity to unearth your own unique story, it presents the challenge to leave a shallow life behind by taking a leap into the abundant life Yeshua offers. 232 Pages

| Paperback | 978-1-7339354-0-1 | $19.99 |

A Life of Favor

A Family Therapist Examines the Story of Joseph and His Brothers
—Rabbi Russell Resnik, MA, LPCC

Favor is an inherent part of God's reality as Father, and properly understood, is a source of blessing to those who want to know him. The story of Jacob's sons points to a life of favor that can make a difference in our lives today. Excellent insight—judgments in exegesis are matched by skillful use of counseling principles and creative applications to contemporary situations in life and in the family. —Walter C. Kaiser, Jr. President Emeritus, Gordon-Conwell Theological Seminary, Hamilton, Mass. 212 Pages

| Paperback | 978-1936716913 | $19.99 |

Will the Nazi Eagle Rise Again?

What the Church Needs to Know about BDS and Other Forces of Anti-Semitism
–David Friedman, Ph.D.

This is the right book at the right time. exposing the roots of Anti-Semitism being resurrected in our days, especially in our Christian Church.
—Dr. Hans-Jörg Kagi, Teacher, Theologian, Basle, Switzerland
Timely and important response to the dangerous hatred of the State of Israel that is growing in society and in the Church. 256 pages

| Paperback | 978-1936716876 | $19.99 |

The Day Jesus Did Tikkun Olam
—Richard A. Robinson, Ph.D.

Easy-to-read, yet scholarly, explores ancient Jewish and Christian scriptures, relevant stories and biblical parallels, to explain the most significant Jewish value—*tikkun olam*—making this world a better place. This is a tenet of both religions, central to the person of Jesus himself. 146 pages
—Murray Tilles, Director, Light of Messiah Ministries; M.Div.
A wealth of scholarship and contemporary relevance with great insight into Jewish ethics and the teachings of Jesus.
—Dr. Richard Harvey, Senior Researcher, Jews for Jesus

| Paperback | 978-1-936716-98-2 | $ 18.99 |

Jewish Giftedness & World Redemption
The Calling of Israel
—Jim Melnick

All things are mortal but the Jew; all other forces pass, but he remains. What is the secret of his immortality?

—Mark Twain, Concerning the Jews, *Harper's Magazine*, September, 1899.

The most comprehensive research of the unique achievements of the Jewish people. The author comes up with the only reason that makes sense of this mystery.

—Daniel C. Juster, Th.D., Restoration from Zion of Tikkun International

Paperback (280 Pages)   978-1-936716-88-3 $24.99

Messianic Judaism *A Modern Movement With an Ancient Past*
—David H. Stern

An updated discussion of the history, ideology, theology and program for Messianic Judaism. A challenge to both Jews and non-Jews who honor Yeshua to catch the vision of Messianic Judaism. 312 pages

Paperback   978-1880226339   **LB62** $17.99

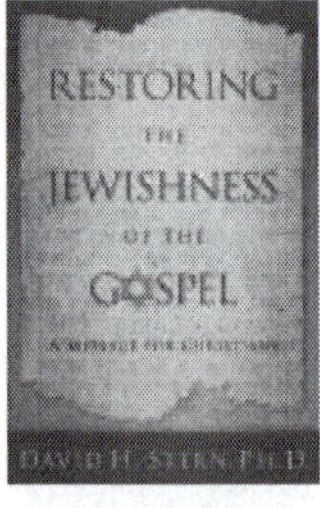

Restoring the Jewishness of the Gospel
A Message for Christians
—David H. Stern

Introduces Christians to the Jewish roots of their faith, challenges some conventional ideas, and raises some neglected questions: How are both the Jews and "the Church" God's people? Is the Law of Moses in force today? Filled with insight! Endorsed by Dr. Darrell L. Bock. 110 pages

English - Paperback	978-1880226667	**LB70**	$9.99
Spanish - Paperback	978-9653590175	**JB14**	$9.99

The Return of the Kosher Pig *The Divine Messiah in Jewish Thought*
—Rabbi Tzahi Shapira

The subject of Messiah fills many pages of rabbinic writings. Hidden in those pages is a little known concept that the Messiah has the same authority given to God. Based on the Scriptures and traditional rabbinic writings, this book shows the deity of Yeshua from a new perspective. You will see that the rabbis of old expected the Messiah to be divine. Softcover, 352 pages.

"One of the most interesting and learned tomes I have ever read. Contained within its pages is much with which I agree, some with which I disagree, and much about which I never thought. Rabbi Shapria's remarkable book cannot be ignored."

—Dr. Paige Patterson, President, Southwest Baptist Theological Seminary

Paperback   978-1936716456   **LB81** $ 39.99

Matthew Presents Yeshua, King Messiah
—Rabbi Barney Kasdan

Few commentators are able to truly present Yeshua in his Jewish context of his background, his family, even his religion. This commentator is well versed with first-century Jewish practices and thought, as well as the historical and cultural setting of the day, and the 'traditions of the Elders' that Yeshua so often spoke about. 448 pages

Paperback	978-1936716265	**LB76**	$29.99

Rabbi Paul Enlightens the Ephesians on Walking with Messiah Yeshua
—Rabbi Barney Kasdan

The Ephesian were a diverse group of Jews and Gentiles, united together in Messiah. They definitely had an impact on the first century world in which they lived. But the Rabbi was not just writing to that local group. What is Paul saying to us? 160 pages.

Paperback	978-11936716821	**LB99**	$17.99

Paul Presents to the Philippians Unity in the Messianic Community
—R. Sean Emslie

A worthy read and an appropriate study for any Messianic Jewish *talmid* or Christian disciple of Yeshua wanting to fairly and faithfully examine apostolic teaching. Emslie's investigation offers a keenly diligent analysis and faithfully responsible apostolic viewpoint. 165 pages

Paperback	978-1733935432 - Coming by June 30, 2020	$18.99

James the Just Presents Application of Torah
—Dr. David Friedman

James (Jacob) one of the Epistles written to first century Jewish followers of Yeshua. Dr. David Friedman, a former Professor of the Israel Bible Institute has shed new light for Christians from this very important letter. 133 pages

Paperback	978-1936716449	**LB82**	$14.99

John's Three Letters on Hope, Love and Covenant Fidelity
—Rabbi Joshua Brumbach

The Letters of John include some of the most beloved and often-quoted portions of scripture. Most people – scholars included – are confident they already have John's letters figured out. But do they really? There is a need for a fresh, post-supersessionist reading of John's letters that challenges common presuppositions regarding their purpose, message and relevance. 168 pages

Paperback	978-1-7339354-6-3 Coming by June 30, 2020	$19.99

Jude On Faith and the Destructive Influence of Heresy
—Rabbi Joshua Brumbach

Almost no other canonical book has been as neglected and overlooked as the Epistle of Jude. This little book may be small, but it has a big message that is even more relevant today as when it was originally written. 100 pages

Paperback	978-1-936716-78-4	**LB97**	$14.99

Yochanan (John) Presents the Revelation of Yeshua the Messiah
—Rabbi Gavriel Lumbroso

The Book of Revelation is perhaps the most mysterious, difficult-to-understand book in all of the Bible. Scholar after scholar, theologian after theologian have wrestled with all the strange visions, images and messages given by Yochanan (John), one of Yeshua's apostles. 206 pages

Paperback	978-1-936716-93-7	$19.99

Psalms & Proverbs *Tehillim* תְּהִלִּים-*Mishlei* מִשְׁלֵי
—Translated by Dr. David Stern

Contemplate the power in these words anytime, anywhere: Psalms-*Tehillim* offers uplifting words of praise and gratitude, keeping us focused with the right attitude; Proverbs-*Mishlei* gives us the wisdom for daily living, renewing our minds by leading us to examine our actions, to discern good from evil, and to decide freely to do the good. Makes a wonderful and meaningful gift. 224 pages.

| Paperback | 978-1936716692 | **LB90** | $9.99 |

At the Feet of Rabbi Gamaliel
Rabbinic Influence in Paul's Teachings
—David Friedman, Ph.D.

Paul (Shaul) was on the "fast track" to becoming a sage and Sanhedrin judge, describing himself as passionate for the Torah and the traditions of the fathers, typical for an aspiring Pharisee: "…trained at the feet of Gamaliel in every detail of the Torah of our forefathers. I was a zealot for God, as all of you are today" (Acts 22.3, CJB). Did Shaul's teachings reflect Rabbi Gamaliel's instructions? Did Paul continue to value the Torah and Pharisaic tradition? Did Paul create a 'New' Theology? The results of the research within these pages and its conclusion may surprise you. 100 pages.

| Paperback | 978-1936716753 | **LB95** | $8.99 |

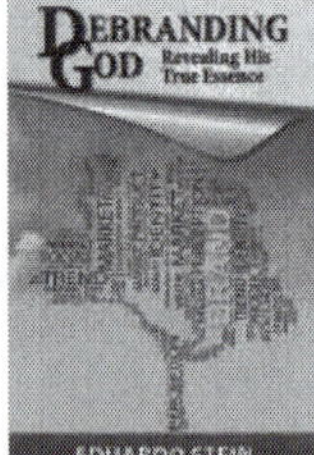

Debranding God *Revealing His True Essence*
—Eduardo Stein

The process of 'debranding' God is to remove all the labels and fads that prompt us to understand him as a supplier and ourselves as the most demanding of customers. Changing our perception of God also changes our perception of ourselves. In knowing who we are in relationship to God, we discover his, and our, true essence. 252 pages.

| Paperback | 978-1936716708 | **LB91** | $16.99 |

Under the Fig Tree *Messianic Thought Through the Hebrew Calendar*
—Patrick Gabriel Lumbroso

Take a daily devotional journey into the Word of God through the Hebrew Calendar and the Biblical Feasts. Learn deeper meaning of the Scriptures through Hebraic thought. Beautifully written and a source for inspiration to draw closer to Adonai every day. 407 pages.

| Paperback | 978-1936716760 | **LB96** | $25.99 |

Under the Vine *Messianic Thought Through the Hebrew Calendar*
—Patrick Gabriel Lumbroso

Journey daily through the Hebrew Calendar and Biblical Feasts into the B'rit Hadashah (New Testament) Scriptures as they are put in their rightful context, bringing Judaism alive in it's full beauty. Messianic faith was the motor and what gave substance to Abraham's new beliefs, hope to Job, trust to Isaac, vision to Jacob, resilience to Joseph, courage to David, wisdom to Solomon, knowledge to Daniel, and divine Messianic authority to Yeshua. 412 pages.

| Paperback | 978-1936716654 | **LB87** | $25.99 |

Come and Worship *Ways to Worship from the Hebrew Scriptures*
—Compiled by Barbara D. Malda

We were created to worship. God has graciously given us many ways to express our praise to him. Each way fits a different situation or moment in life, yet all are intended to bring honor and glory to him. When we believe that he is who he says he is [see *His Names are Wonderful!*] and that his Word is true, worship flows naturally from our hearts to his. 128 pages.

Paperback	978-1936716678	**LB88**	$9.99

His Names Are Wonderful

Getting to Know God Through His Hebrew Names

—Elizabeth L. Vander Meulen and Barbara D. Malda

In Hebrew thought, names did more than identify people; they revealed their nature. God's identity is expressed not in one name, but in many. This book will help readers know God better as they uncover the truths in his Hebrew names. 160 pages.

Paperback	978-1880226308	**LB58**	$9.99

The Revolt of Rabbi Morris Cohen

Exploring the Passion & Piety of a Modern-day Pharisee
—Anthony Cardinale

A brilliant school psychologist, Rabbi Morris Cohen went on a one-man strike to protest the systematic mislabeling of slow learning pupils as "Learning Disabled" (to extract special education money from the state). His disciplinary hearing, based on the transcript, is a hilarious read! This effusive, garrulous man with an irresistible sense of humor lost his job, but achieved a major historic victory causing the reform of the billion-dollar special education program. Enter into the mind of an eighth-generation Orthodox rabbi to see how he deals spiritually with the loss of everything, even the love of his children. This modern-day Pharisee discovered a trusted friend in the author (a born again believer in Jesus) with whom he could openly struggle over Rabbinic Judaism as well as the concept of Jesus (Yeshua) as Messiah. 320 pages.

Paperback	978-1936716722	**LB92**	$19.99

Stories of Yeshua

—Jim Reimann, Illustrator Julia Filipone-Erez

Children's Bible Storybook with four stories about Yeshua (Jesus).
Yeshua is Born: The Bethlehem Story based on Lk 1:26-35 & 2:1-20; *Yeshua and Nicodemus in Jerusalem* based on Jn 3:1-16; *Yeshua Loves the Little Children of the World* based on Matthew 18:1–6 & 19:13–15; *Yeshua is Alive-The Empty Tomb in Jerusalem* based on Matthew 26:17-56, Jn 19:16-20:18, Lk 24:50-53. Ages 3-7, 48 pages.

Paperback	978-1936716685	**LB89**	$14.99

To the Ends of the Earth – How the First Jewish Followers of Yeshua Transformed the Ancient World
— Dr. Jeffrey Seif

Everyone knows that the first followers of Yeshua were Jews, and that Christianity was very Jewish for the first 50 to 100 years. It's a known fact that there were many congregations made up mostly of Jews, although the false perception today is, that in the second century they disappeared. Dr. Seif reveals the truth of what happened to them and how these early Messianic Jews influenced and transformed the behavior of the known world at that time. 171 pages

Paperback	978-1936716463	**LB83**	$17.99

Jewish Roots and Foundations of the Scriptures I & II
—John Fischer, Th.D, Ph.D.

An outstanding evangelical leader once said: "There is something shallow about a Christianity that has lost its Jewish roots." A beautiful painting is a careful interweaving of a number of elements. Among other things, there are the background, the foreground and the subject. Discovering the roots of your faith is a little like appreciating the various parts of a painting. In the background is the panorama of preparation and pictures found in the Old Testament. In the foreground is the landscape and light of the first century Jewish setting. All of this is intricately connected with and highlights the subject—which becomes the flowering of all these aspects—the coming of God to earth and what that means for us. Discovering and appreciating your roots in this way broadens, deepens and enriches your faith and your understanding of Scripture. This audio is 32 hours of live class instruction - audio is clear and easy to understand.

9781936716623   **LCD03 / LCD04** $49.99 each

The Gospels in their Jewish Context
—John Fischer, Th.D, Ph.D.

An examination of the Jewish background and nature of the Gospels in their contemporary political, cultural and historical settings, emphasizing each gospel's special literary presentation of Yeshua, and highlighting the cultural and religious contexts necessary for understanding each of the gospels. 32 hours of audio/video instruction on MP3-DVD and pdf of syllabus.

978-1936716241   **LCD01** $49.99

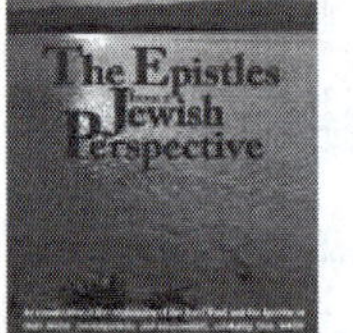

The Epistles from a Jewish Perspective
—John Fischer, Th.D, Ph.D.

An examination of the relationship of Rabbi Shaul (the Apostle Paul) and the Apostles to their Jewish contemporaries and environment; surveys their Jewish practices, teaching, controversy with the religious leaders, and many critical passages, with emphasis on the Jewish nature, content, and background of these letters. 32 hours of audio/video instruction on MP3-DVD and pdf of syllabus.

978-1936716258   **LCD02** $49.99

The Red Heifer *A Jewish Cry for Messiah*
—Anthony Cardinale

Award-winning journalist and playwright Anthony Cardinale has traveled extensively in Israel, and recounts here his interviews with Orthodox rabbis, secular Israelis, and Palestinian Arabs about the current search for a red heifer by Jewish radicals wishing to rebuild the Temple and bring the Messiah. These real-life interviews are interwoven within an engaging and dramatic fictional portrayal of the diverse people of Israel and how they would react should that red heifer be found. Readers will find themselves in the Land, where they can hear learned rabbis and ordinary Israelis talking about the red heifer and dealing with all the related issues and the imminent coming and identity of Messiah. 341 pages

Paperback   978-1936716470   **LB79** $19.99

The Borough Park Papers
—Multiple Authors

As you read the New Testament, you "overhear" debates first-century Messianic Jews had about critical issues, e.g. Gentiles being "allowed" into the Messianic kingdom (Acts 15). Similarly, you're now invited to "listen in" as leading twenty-first century Messianic Jewish theologians discuss critical issues facing us today. Some ideas may not fit into your previously held pre-suppositions or pre-conceptions. Indeed, you may find some paradigm shifting in your thinking. We want to share the thoughts of these thinkers with you, our family in the Messiah.

Symposium I:
The Gospel and the Jewish People

248 pages, Paperback   978-1936716593   **LB84** $39.95

Symposium II:
The Deity of Messiah and the Mystery of God

211 pages, Paperback   978-1936716609   **LB85** $39.95

Symposium III:
How Jewish Should the Messianic Community Be?

Paperback   978-1936716616   **LB86** $39.95

Passion for Israel: *A Short History of the Evangelical Church's Support of Israel and the Jewish People*
—Dan Juster

History reveals a special commitment of Christians to the Jews as God's still elect people, but the terrible atrocities committed against the Jews by so-called Christians have overshadowed the many good deeds that have been performed. This important history needs to be told to help heal the wounds and to inspire more Christians to stand together in support of Israel. 84 pages

Paperback   978-1936716401   **LB78** $9.99

On The Way to Emmaus: *Searching the Messianic Prophecies*
—Dr. Jacques Doukhan

An outstanding compilation of the most critical Messianic prophecies by a renowned conservative Christian Scholar, drawing on material from the Bible, Rabbinic sources, Dead Sea Scrolls, and more. 217 pages

Paperback   978-1936716432   **LB80** $14.99

Yeshua *A Guide to the Real Jesus and the Original Church*
—Dr. Ron Moseley

Opens up the history of the Jewish roots of the Christian faith. Illuminates the Jewish background of Yeshua and the Church and never flinches from showing "Jesus was a Jew, who was born, lived, and died, within first century Judaism." Explains idioms in the New Testament. Endorsed by Dr. Brad Young and Dr. Marvin Wilson. 213 pages.

Paperback   978-1880226681   **LB29** $12.99

Gateways to Torah *Joining the Ancient Conversation on the Weekly Portion*
—Rabbi Russell Resnik

From before the days of Messiah until today, Jewish people have read from and discussed a prescribed portion of the Pentateuch each week. Now, a Messianic Jewish Rabbi, Russell Resnik, brings another perspective on the Torah, that of a Messianic Jew. 246 pages.

Paperback	978-1880226889	**LB42**	$15.99

Creation to Completion *A Guide to Life's Journey from the Five Books of Moses*
—Rabbi Russell Resnik

Endorsed by Coach Bill McCartney, Founder of Promise Keepers & Road to Jerusalem: "Paul urged Timothy to study the Scriptures (2 Tim. 3:16), advising him to apply its teachings to all aspects of his life. Since there was no New Testament then, this rabbi/apostle was convinced that his disciple would profit from studying the Torah, the Five Books of Moses, and the Old Testament. Now, Rabbi Resnik has written a warm devotional commentary that will help you understand and apply the Law of Moses to your life in a practical way." 256 pages

Paperback	978-1880226322	**LB61**	$14.99

Walk Genesis! Walk Exodus! Walk Leviticus! Walk Numbers! Walk Deuteronomy!
Messianic Jewish Devotional Commentaries
—Jeffrey Enoch Feinberg, Ph.D.

Using the weekly synagogue readings, Dr. Jeffrey Feinberg has put together some very valuable material in his "Walk" series. Each section includes a short Hebrew lesson (for the non-Hebrew speaker), key concepts, an excellent overview of the portion, and some practical applications. Can be used as a daily devotional as well as a Bible study tool.Paperback.

Walk Genesis!	238 pages	978-1880226759	**LB34**	$12.99
Walk Exodus!	224 pages	978-1880226872	**LB40**	$12.99
Walk Leviticus!	208 pages	978-1880226926	**LB45**	$12.99
Walk Numbers!	211 pages	978-1880226995	**LB48**	$12.99
Walk Deuteronomy!	231 pages	978-1880226186	**LB51**	$12.99
SPECIAL! Five-book Walk!		5 Book Set **Save $10**	**LK28**	$54.99

Good News According To Matthew

—Dr. Henry Einspruch

English translation with quotations from the Tanakh (Old Testament) capitalized and printed in Hebrew. Helpful notations are included. Lovely black and white illustrations throughout the book. 86 pages.

Paperback	978-1880226025	**LB03**	$4.99
Also available in Yiddish.		**LB02**	$4.99

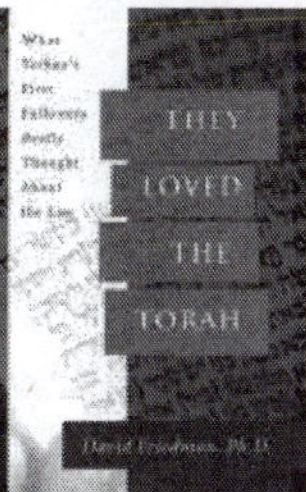

They Loved the Torah *What Yeshua's First Followers Really Thought About the Law*

—Dr. David Friedman

Although many Jews believe that Paul taught against the Law, this book disproves that notion. An excellent case for his premise that all the first followers of the Messiah were not only Torah-observant, but also desired to spread their love for God's entire Word to the gentiles to whom they preached. 144 pages. Endorsed by Dr. David Stern, Ariel Berkowitz, Rabbi Dr. Stuart Dauermann & Dr. John Fischer.

Paperback	978-1880226940	**LB47**	$9.99

The Distortion *2000 Years of Misrepresenting the Relationship Between Jesus the Messiah and the Jewish People*

—Dr. John Fischer & Dr. Patrice Fischer

Did the Jews kill Jesus? Did they really reject him? With the rise of global anti–Semitism, it is important to understand what the Gospels teach about the relationship between Jewish people and their Messiah. 2000 years of distortion have made this difficult. Learn how the distortion began and continues to this day and what you can do to change it. 126 pages. Endorsed by Dr. Ruth Fleischer, Rabbi Russell Resnik, Dr. Daniel C. Juster, Dr. Michael Rydelnik.

Paperback	978-1880226254	**LB54**	$11.99

eBooks Now Available!

Versions available for your favorite reader

Visit www.messianicjewish.net for direct links to these readers for each available eBook.

God's Appointed Times *A Practical Guide to Understanding and Celebrating the Biblical Holidays –* **New Edition.**
—Rabbi Barney Kasdan

The Biblical Holy Days teach us about the nature of God and his plan for mankind, and can be a source of God's blessing for all believers–Jews and Gentiles–today. Includes historical background, traditional Jewish observance, New Testament relevance, and prophetic significance, plus music, crafts and holiday recipes. 145 pages.

English - Paperback	978-1880226353	**LB63**	$12.99
Spanish - Paperback	978-1880226391	**LB59**	$12.99

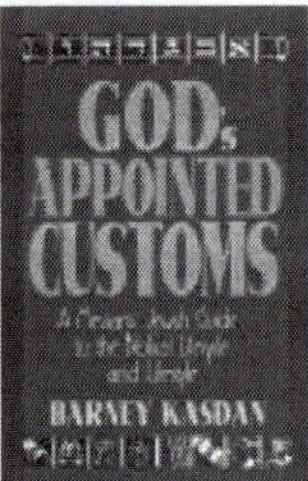

God's Appointed Customs *A Messianic Jewish Guide to the Biblical Lifecycle and Lifestyle*
— Rabbi Barney Kasdan

Explains how biblical customs are often the missing key to unlocking the depths of Scripture. Discusses circumcision, the Jewish wedding, and many more customs mentioned in the New Testament. Companion to *God's Appointed Times*. 170 pages.

English - Paperback	978-1880226636	**LB26**	$12.99
Spanish - Paperback	978-1880226551	**LB60**	$12.99

Celebrations of the Bible *A Messianic Children's Curriculum*

Did you know that each Old Testament feast or festival finds its fulfillment in the New? They enrich the lives of people who experience and enjoy them. Our popular curriculum for children is in a brand new, user-friendly format. The lay-flat at binding allows you to easily reproduce handouts and worksheets. Celebrations of the Bible has been used by congregations, Sunday schools, ministries, homeschoolers, and individuals to teach children about the biblical festivals. Each of these holidays are presented for Preschool (2-K), Primary (Grades 1-3), Junior (Grades 4-6), and Children's Worship/Special Services. 208 pages.

Paperback	978-1880226261	**LB55**	$24.99

Passover: *The Key That Unlocks the Book of Revelation*
—Daniel C. Juster, Th.D.

Is there any more enigmatic book of the Bible than Revelation? Controversy concerning its meaning has surrounded it back to the first century. Today, the arguments continue. Yet, Dan Juster has given us the key that unlocks the entire book—the events and circumstances of the Passover/Exodus. By interpreting Revelation through the lens of Exodus, Dan Juster provides a unified overview that helps us read Revelation as it was always meant to be read, as a drama of spiritual conflict, deliverance, and above all, worship. He also shows how this final drama, fulfilled in Messiah, resonates with the Torah and all of God's Word. — Russ Resnik, Executive Director, Union of Messianic Jewish Congregations.

Paperback	978-1936716210	**LB74**	$10.99

The Messianic Passover Haggadah
Revised and Updated
—Rabbi Barry Rubin and Steffi Rubin.

Guides you through the traditional Passover seder dinner, step-by-step. Not only does this observance remind us of our rescue from Egyptian bondage, but, we remember Messiah's last supper, a Passover seder. The theme of redemption is seen throughout the evening. What's so unique about our Haggadah is the focus on Yeshua (Jesus) the Messiah and his teaching, especially on his last night in the upper room. 36 pages.

English - Paperback	978-1880226292	**LB57**	$4.99
Spanish - Paperback	978-1880226599	**LBSP01**	$4.99

The Messianic Passover Seder Preparation Guide
Includes recipes, blessings and songs. 19 pages.

English - Paperback	978-1880226247	**LB10**	$2.99
Spanish - Paperback	978-1880226728	**LBSP02**	$2.99

The Sabbath *Entering God's Rest*
—Barry Rubin & Steffi Rubin

Even if you've never celebrated Shabbat before, this book will guide you into the rest God has for all who would enter in—Jews and non-Jews. Contains prayers, music, recipes; in short, everything you need to enjoy the Sabbath, even how to observe havdalah, the closing ceremony of the Sabbath. Also discusses the Saturday or Sunday controversy. 48 pages.

Paperback	978-1880226742	**LB32**	$6.99

Havdalah *The Ceremony that Completes the Sabbath*
—Dr. Neal & Jamie Lash

The Sabbath ends with this short, yet equally sweet ceremony called havdalah (separation). This ceremony reminds us to be a light and a sweet fragrance in this world of darkness as we carry the peace, rest, joy and love of the Sabbath into the work week. 28 pages.

Paperback	978-1880226605	**LB69**	$4.99

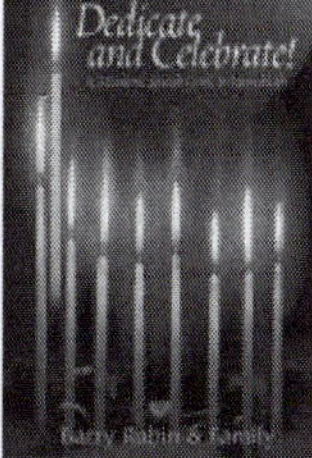

Dedicate and Celebrate!
A Messianic Jewish Guide to Hanukkah
—Barry Rubin & Family

Hanukkah means "dedication" — a theme of significance for Jews and Christians. Discussing its historical background, its modern-day customs, deep meaning for all of God's people, this little book covers all the how-tos! Recipes, music, and prayers for lighting the menorah, all included! 32 pages.

Paperback	978-1880226834	**LB36**	$4.99

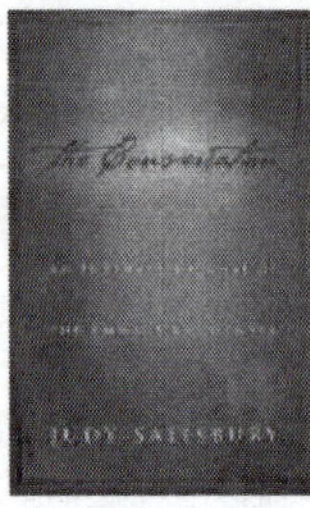

The Conversation
An Intimate Journal of the Emmaus Encounter
—Judy Salisbury

"Then beginning with Moses and with all the prophets, He explained to them the things concerning Himself in all the Scriptures." Luke 24:27
If you've ever wondered what that conversation must have been like, this captivating book takes you there.
"The Conversation brings to life that famous encounter between the two disciples and our Lord Jesus on the road to Emmaus. While it is based in part on an imaginative reconstruction, it is filled with the throbbing pulse of the excitement of the sensational impact that our Lord's resurrection should have on all of our lives." ~ Dr. Walter Kaiser President Emeritus Gordon-Conwell Theological Seminary. Hardcover 120 pages.

Hardcover	978-1936716173	**LB73**	$14.99
Paperback	978-1936716364	**LB77**	$9.99

Growing to Maturity
A Messianic Jewish Discipleship Guide
—Daniel C. Juster, Th.D.

This discipleship series presents first steps of understanding and spiritual practice, tailored for the Jewish believer. It's purpose is to aid the believer in living according to Yeshua's will as a disciple, one who has learned the example of his teacher. The course is structured according to recent advances in individualized educational instruction. Discipleship is serious business and the material is geared for serious study and reflection. Each chapter is divided into short sections followed by study questions. 256 pages.

Paperback	978-1936716227	**LB75**	$19.99

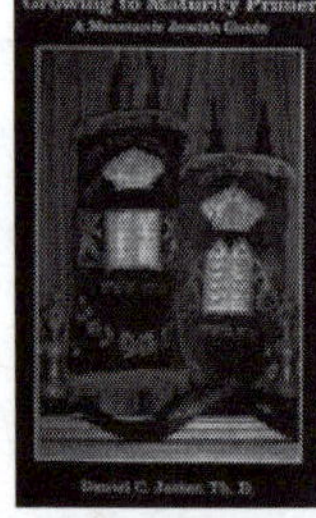

Growing to Maturity Primer: *A Messianic Jewish Discipleship Workbook*
—Daniel C. Juster, Th.D.

A basic book of material in question and answer form. Usable by everyone. 60 pages.

Paperback	978-0961455507	**TB16**	$7.99

Conveying Our Heritage A Messianic Jewish Guide to Home Practice
—Daniel C. Juster, Th.D. Patricia A. Juster

Throughout history the heritage of faith has been conveyed within the family and the congregation. The first institution in the Bible is the family and only the family can raise children with an adequate appreciation of our faith and heritage. This guide exists to help families learn how to pass on the heritage of spiritual Messianic Jewish life. Softcover, 86 pages

Paperback	978-1936716739	**LB93**	$8.99

That They May Be One *A Brief Review of Church Restoration Movements and Their Connection to the Jewish People*
—Daniel Juster, Th.D

Something prophetic and momentous is happening. The Church is finally fully grasping its relationship to Israel and the Jewish people. Author describes the restoration movements in Church history and how they connected to Israel and the Jewish people. Each one contributed in some way—some more, some less—toward the ultimate unity between Jews and Gentiles. Predicted in the Old Testament and fulfilled in the New, Juster believes this plan of God finds its full expression in Messianic Judaism. He may be right. See what you think as you read *That They May Be One*. 100 pages.

Paperback	978-1880226711	**LB71**	$9.99

The Greatest Commandment
How the Sh'ma Leads to More Love in Your Life
—Irene Lipson

"What is the greatest commandment?" Yeshua was asked. His reply—"Hear, O Israel, the Lord our God, the Lord is one, and you are to love Adonai your God with all your heart, with all your soul, with all your understanding, and all your strength." A superb book explaining each word so the meaning can be fully grasped and lived. Endorsed by Elliot Klayman, Susan Perlman, & Robert Stearns. 175 pages.

Paperback	978-1880226360	**LB65**	$12.99

Blessing the King of the Universe
Transforming Your Life Through the Practice of Biblical Praise
—Irene Lipson

Insights into the ancient biblical practice of blessing God are offered clearly and practically. With examples from Scripture and Jewish tradition, this book teaches the biblical formula used by men and women of the Bible, including the Messiah; points to new ways and reasons to praise the Lord; and explains more about the Jewish roots of the faith. Endorsed by Rabbi Barney Kasdan, Dr. Mitch Glaser, & Rabbi Dr. Dan Cohn-Sherbok. 144 pages.

Paperback	978-1880226797	**LB53**	$11.99

You Bring the Bagels, I'll Bring the Gospel
Sharing the Messiah with Your Jewish Neighbor
Revised Edition—Now with Study Questions
—Rabbi Barry Rubin

This "how-to-witness-to-Jewish-people" book is an orderly presentation of everything you need to share the Messiah with a Jewish friend. Includes Messianic prophecies, Jewish objections to believing, sensitivities in your witness, words to avoid. A "must read" for all who care about the Jewish people. Good for individual or group study. Used in Bible schools. Endorsed by Harold A. Sevener, Dr. Walter C. Kaiser, Dr. Erwin J. Kolb and Dr. Arthur F. Glasser. 253 pages, Paperback.

English	978-1880226650	**LB13**	$12.99
Te Tengo Buenas Noticias	978-0829724103	**OBSP02**	$14.99

Making Eye Contact With God

A Weekly Devotional for Women

—Terri Gillespie

What kind of eyes do you have? Are they downcast and sad? Are they full of God's joy and passion? See yourself through the eyes of God. Using real life anecdotes, combined with scripture, the author reveals God's heart for women everywhere, as she softly speaks of the ways in which women see God. Endorsed by prominent authors: Dr. Angela Hunt, Wanda Dyson and Kathryn Mackel. 247 pages.

Hardcover   978-1880226513   **LB68** $19.99

Divine Reversal

The Transforming Ethics of Jesus

—Rabbi Russell Resnik

In the Old Testament, God often reversed the plans of man. Yeshua's ethics continue this theme. Following his path transforms one's life from within, revealing the source of true happiness, forgiveness, reconciliation, fidelity and love. From the introduction, "As a Jewish teacher, Jesus doesn't separate matters of theology from practice. His teaching is consistently practical, ethical, and applicable to real life, even two thousand years after it was originally given." Endorsed by Jonathan Bernis, Dr. Daniel C. Juster, Dr. Jeffrey L. Seif, and Dr Darrell Bock. 206 pages

Paperback   978-1880226803   **LB72** $12.99

Praying Like the Jew, Jesus

Recovering the Ancient Roots of New Testament Prayer

—Dr. Timothy P. Jones

This eye-opening book reveals the Jewish background of many of Yeshua's prayers. Historical vignettes "transport" you to the times of Yeshua so you can grasp the full meaning of Messiah's prayers. Unique devotional thoughts and meditations, presented in down-to-earth language, provide inspiration for a more meaningful prayer life and help you draw closer to God. Endorsed by Mark Galli, James W. Goll, Rev. Robert Stearns, James F. Strange, and Dr. John Fischer. 144 pages.

Paperback   978-1880226285   **LB56** $9.99

Growing Your Olive Tree Marriage *A Guide for Couples from Two Traditions*

—David J. Rudolph

One partner is Jewish; the other is Christian. Do they celebrate Hanukkah, Christmas or both? Do they worship in a church or a synagogue? How will the children be raised? This is the first book from a biblical perspective that addresses the concerns of intermarried couples, offering a godly solution. Includes highlights of interviews with intermarried couples. Endorsed by Walter C. Kaiser, Jr., Rabbi Dan Cohn-Sherbok, Jonathan Settel, Dr. Mitchell Glaser & Natalie Sirota. 224 pages.

Paperback   978-1880226179   **LB50** $12.99

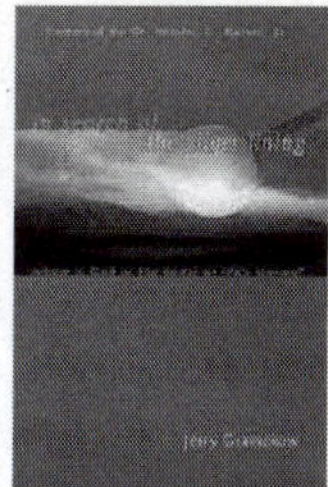

In Search of the Silver Lining *Where is God in the Midst of Life's Storms?*
—Jerry Gramckow

When faced with suffering, what are your choices? Storms have always raged. And people have either perished in their wake or risen above the tempests, shaping history by their responses…new storms are on the horizon. How will we deal with them? How will we shape history or those who follow us? The answer lies in how we view God in the midst of the storms. Endorsed by Joseph C. Aldrich, Ray Beeson, Dr. Daniel Juster. 176 pages.

| Paperback | 978-1880226865 | **LB39** | $10.99 |

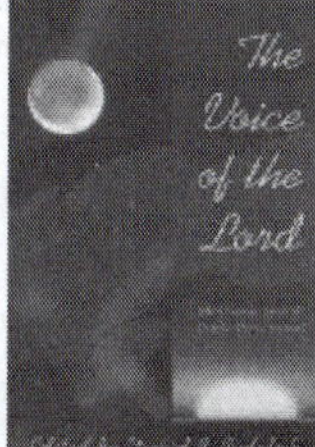

The Voice of the Lord *Messianic Jewish Daily Devotional*
—Edited by David J. Rudolph

Brings insight into the Jewish Scriptures—both Old and New Testaments. Twenty-two prominent Messianic contributors provide practical ways to apply biblical truth. Start your day with this unique resource. Explanatory notes. Perfect companion to the Complete Jewish Bible (see page 2). Endorsed by Edith Schaeffer, Dr. Arthur F. Glaser, Dr. Michael L. Brown, Mitch Glaser and Moishe Rosen. 416 pages.

| Paperback | 9781880226704 | **LB31** | $19.99 |

Kingdom Relationships *God's Laws for the Community of Faith*
—Dr. Ron Moseley

Dr. Ron Moseley's Yeshua: A Guide to the Real Jesus and the Original Church has taught thousands of people about the Jewishness of not only Yeshua, but of the first followers of the Messiah.

In this work, Moseley focuses on the teaching of Torah -- the Five Books of Moses -- tapping into truths that greatly help modern-day members of the community of faith. 64 pages.

| Paperback | 978-1880226841 | **LB37** | $8.99 |

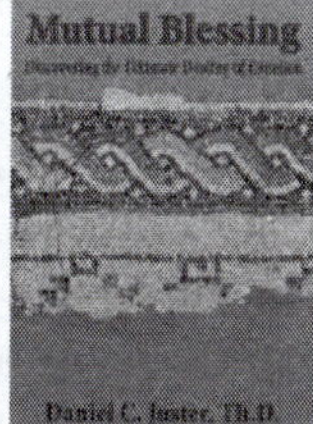

Mutual Blessing *Discovering the Ultimate Destiny of Creation*
—Daniel C. Juster

To truly love as God loves is to see the wonder and richness of the distinct differences in all of creation and his natural order of interdependence. This is the way to mutual blessing and the discovery of the ultimate destiny of creation. Learn how to become enriched and blessed as you enrich and bless others and all that is around you! Softcover, 135 pages.

| Paperback | 978-1936716746 | **LB94** | $9.99 |

Train Up A Child *Successful Parenting For The Next Generation*
—Dr. Daniel L. Switzer

The author, former principal of Ets Chaiyim Messianic Jewish Day School, and father of four, combines solid biblical teaching with Jewish sources on child raising, focusing on the biblical holy days, giving fresh insight into fulfilling the role of parent. 188 pages. Endorsed by Dr. David J. Rudolph, Paul Lieberman, and Dr. David H. Stern.

| Paperback | 978-1880226377 | **LB64** | $12.99 |

Fire on the Mountain - *Past Renewals, Present Revivals and the Coming Return of Israel*
—Dr. Louis Goldberg

The term "revival" is often used to describe a person or congregation turning to God. Is this something that "just happens," or can it be brought about? Dr. Louis Goldberg, author and former professor of Hebrew and Jewish Studies at Moody Bible Institute, examines real revivals that took place in Bible times and applies them to today. 268 pages.

| Paperback | 978-1880226858 | **LB38** | $15.99 |

Voices of Messianic Judaism *Confronting Critical Issues Facing a Maturing Movement*
—General Editor Rabbi Dan Cohn-Sherbok

Many of the best minds of the Messianic Jewish movement contributed their thoughts to this collection of 29 substantive articles. Challenging questions are debated: The involvement of Gentiles in Messianic Judaism? How should outreach be accomplished? Liturgy or not? Intermarriage? 256 pages.

| Paperback | 978-1880226933 | **LB46** | $15.99 |

The Enduring Paradox *Exploratory Essays in Messianic Judaism*
—General Editor Dr. John Fischer

Yeshua and his Jewish followers began a new movement—Messianic Judaism—2,000 years ago. In the 20th century, it was reborn. Now, at the beginning of the 21st century, it is maturing. Twelve essays from top contributors to the theology of this vital movement of God, including: Dr. Walter C. Kaiser, Dr. David H. Stern, and Dr. John Fischer. 196 pages.

| Paperback | 978-1880226902 | **LB43** | $13.99 |

The World To Come *A Portal to Heaven on Earth*
—Derek Leman

An insightful book, exposing fallacies and false teachings surrounding this extremely important subject... paints a hopeful picture of the future and dispels many non-biblical notions. Intriguing chapters: Magic and Desire, The Vision of the Prophets, Hints of Heaven, Horrors of Hell, The Drama of the Coming Ages. Offers a fresh, but old, perspective on the world to come, as it interacts with the prophets of Israel and the Bible. 110 pages.

| Paperback | 978-1880226049 | **LB67** | $9.99 |

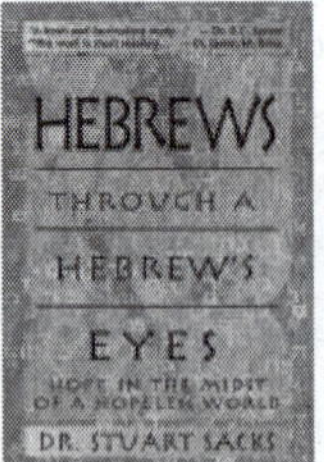

Hebrews Through a Hebrew's Eyes
—Dr. Stuart Sacks

Written to first-century Messianic Jews, this epistle, understood through Jewish eyes, edifies and encourages all. 119 pages. Endorsed by Dr. R.C. Sproul and James M. Boice.

| Paperback | 978-1880226612 | **LB23** | $10.99 |

The Irrevocable Calling *Israel's Role As A Light To The Nations*
—Daniel C. Juster, Th.D.

Referring to the chosen-ness of the Jewish people, Paul, the Apostle, wrote "For God's free gifts and his calling are irrevocable" (Rom. 11:29). This messenger to the Gentiles understood the unique calling of his people, Israel. So does Dr. Daniel Juster, President of Tikkun Ministries Int'l. In *The Irrevocable Calling*, he expands Paul's words, showing how Israel was uniquely chosen to bless the world and how these blessings can be enjoyed today. Endorsed by Dr. Jack Hayford, Mike Bickle and Don Finto. 64 pages.

| Paperback | 978-1880226346 | **LB66** | $8.99 |

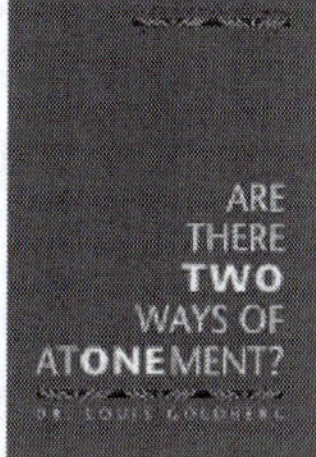

Are There Two Ways of Atonement?
—Dr. Louis Goldberg

Here Dr. Louis Goldberg, long-time professor of Jewish Studies at Moody Bible Institute, exposes the dangerous doctrine of Two-Covenant Theology. 32 pages.

| Paperback | 978-1880226056 | **LB12** | $ 4.99 |

Awakening *Articles and Stories About Jews and Yeshua*
—Arranged by Anna Portnov

Articles, testimonies, and stories about Jewish people and their relationship with God, Israel, and the Messiah. Includes the effective tract, "The Most Famous Jew of All." One of our best anthologies for witnessing to Jewish people. Let this book witness for you! Russian version also available. 110 pages.

| English - Paperback | 978-1880226094 | **LB15** | $ 6.99 |
| Russian - Paperback | 978-1880226018 | **LB14** | $ 6.99 |

The Unpromised Land *The Struggle of Messianic Jews Gary and Shirley Beresford*
—Linda Alexander

They felt God calling them to live in Israel, the Promised Land. Wanting nothing more than to live quietly and grow old together in the country of refuge for all Jewish people, little did they suspect what events would follow to try their faith. The fight to make *aliyah*, to claim their rightful inheritance in the Promised Land, became a battle waged not only for themselves, but also for Messianic Jews all over the world that wish to return to the Jewish homeland. Here is the true saga of the Beresford`s journey to the land of their forefathers. 216 pages.

| Paperback | 978-1880226568 | **LB19** | $ 9.99 |

Death of Messiah *Twenty fascinating articles that address a subject of grief, hope, and ultimate triumph.*
—Edited by Kai Kjaer-Hansen

This compilation, written by well-known Jewish believers, addresses the issue of Messiah and offers proof that Yeshua—the true Messiah—not only died, but also was resurrected! 160 pages.

Paperback   978-1880226582   **LB20** $ 8.99

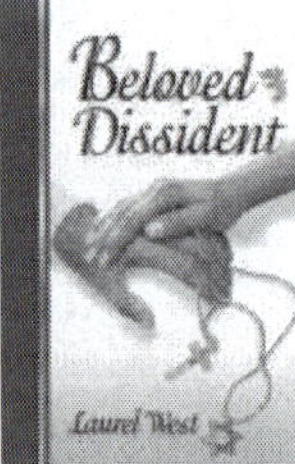

Beloved Dissident *(A Novel)*
—Laurel West

A gripping story of human relationships, passionate love, faith, and spiritual testing. Set in the world of high finance, intrigue, and international terrorism, the lives of David, Jonathan, and Leah intermingle on many levels--especially their relationships with one another and with God. As the two men tangle with each other in a rising whirlwind of excitement and danger, each hopes to win the fight for Leah's love. One of these rivals will move Leah to a level of commitment and love she has never imagined--or dared to dream. Whom will she choose? 256 pages.

Paperback   978-1880226766   **LB33** $ 9.99

Sudden Terror
—Dr. David Friedman

Exposes the hidden agenda of militant Islam. The author, a former member of the Israel Defense Forces, provides eye-opening information needed in today's dangerous world.

Dr. David Friedman recounts his experiences confronting terrorism; analyzes the biblical roots of the conflict between Israel and Islam; provides an overview of early Islam; demonstrates how the United States and Israel are bound together by a common enemy; and shows how to cope with terrorism and conquer fear. The culmination of many years of research and personal experiences. This expose will prepare you for what's to come! 160 pages.

Paperback   978-1880226155   **LB49** $ 9.99

It is Good! *Growing Up in a Messianic Family*
—Steffi Rubin

Growing up in a Messianic Jewish family. Meet Tovah! Tovah (Hebrew for "Good") is growing up in a Messianic Jewish home, learning the meaning of God's special days. Ideal for young children, it teaches the biblical holidays and celebrates faith in Yeshua. 32 pages to read & color.

Paperback   978-1880226063   **LB11** $ 4.99
